JOURNAL FOR THE STUDY OF THE OLD TESTAMENT SUPPLEMENT SERIES

10

Sheffield Academic Pr

BY THE SAME AUTHOR

I, He, We and They: A Literary Approach to Isaiah 53 (JSOT Press, 1976)
The Theme of the Pentateuch (JSOT Press, 1978)
Ezra, Nehemiah, Esther (Marshall, Morgan & Scott, and Eerdmans, 1984)
The Esther Scroll: The Story of the Story (JSOT Press, 1984)
What Does Eve Do to Help? and Other Readerly Questions to the Old Testament (JSOT Press, 1990)
Job 1–20 (Word Books, 1990)
Interested Parties: The Ideology of Writers and Readers of the Hebrew Bible (Sheffield Academic Press, 1995)
The Bible and the Modern World (Sheffield Academic Press, 1997)
The Sheffield Style Manual for Authors and Editors in Biblical Studies (Sheffield Academic Press, 1997)

EDITED BOOKS

Art and Meaning: Rhetoric in Biblical Literature (ed. David J.A. Clines, David M. Gunn and Alan J. Hauser; JSOT Press, 1982)
Midian, Moab and Edom: The History and Archaeology of Late Bronze and Iron Age Jordan and North-West Arabia (ed. John F.A. Sawyer and David J.A. Clines; JSOT Press, 1983)
The Bible in Three Dimensions: Essays in Celebration of the Fortieth Anniversary of the Department of Biblical Studies in the University of Sheffield (ed. David J.A. Clines, Stephen E. Fowl and Stanley E. Porter; JSOT Press, 1990)
Telling Queen Michal's Story: An Experiment in Comparative Interpretation (ed. David J.A. Clines and Tamara C. Eskenazi; JSOT Press, 1991)
Among the Prophets: Imagery, Language and Structure in the Prophetic Writings (ed. Philip R. Davies and David J.A. Clines; JSOT Press, 1993)
Of Prophets' Visions and the Wisdom of Sages: Essays in Honour of R. Norman Whybray on his Seventieth Birthday (ed. Heather A. McKay and David J.A. Clines; JSOT Press, 1993)
The New Literary Criticism and the Hebrew Bible (ed. J. Cheryl Exum and David J.A. Clines; JSOT Press, 1993)
The Dictionary of Classical Hebrew. I. *Aleph* (Sheffield Academic Press, 1993)
The Dictionary of Classical Hebrew. II. *Beth–Waw* (Sheffield Academic Press, 1995)
The Bible in Human Society: Essays in Honour of John Rogerson (ed. R. Daniel Carroll R., David J.A. Clines and Philip R. Davies; Sheffield Academic Press, 1995)
The Dictionary of Classical Hebrew. III. *Zayin–Teth* (Sheffield Academic Press, 1996)
The Poetical Books (Sheffield Academic Press, 1997)

The Theme of the Pentateuch

Second Edition

David J.A. Clines

Journal for the Study of the Old Testament
Supplement Series, 10

1997
Sheffield

To my mother
and to the memory of my father,
from a far country

First published by JSOT Press 1978
Reprinted 1982, 1984, 1986, 1989, 1992, 1994

Second Edition, Sheffield Academic Press, 1997

Published by
Sheffield Academic Press

Printed and bound in Great Britain by

The Cromwell Press
Melksham, Wiltshire

British Library Cataloguing in Publication Data

A catalogue record for this book is available
from the British Library

ISBN 1-85075-792-5 (paperback)

Contents

Preface

In this book I am arguing that the Pentateuch is a unity—not in origin, but in its final shape. Two centuries of Biblical criticism have trained us to look for unity, if at all, in the Pentateuch's sources rather than in the final product. I have thought it worthwhile to suggest that it is time that we ignored the sources—hypothetical as they are—for a little, and asked what the Pentateuch as a whole is about; that is to say, what is its theme.

My thanks are due to the Research Fund Committee of the University of Sheffield for financial assistance toward the typing of the manuscript, and to the editor of the *Catholic Biblical Quarterly* for permission to incorporate in a revised form material on the theme of Genesis 1–11 which I published in that journal *(CBQ* 38 [1976], pp. 483-507). I am grateful for a number of helpful criticisms made by members of the Society for Old Testament Study, to whom an embryonic form of this monograph was read as a paper in July, 1977. I value particularly the generous encouragement of Brevard Childs, who spent some of his precious sabbatical in Britain in reading and discussing my paper with me. Lastly, I must acknowledge the unfailing support of my colleagues David Gunn and Philip Davies, whose confidence in me in accepting this book into the Supplement Series of the *Journal for the Study of the Old Testament* I greatly appreciate.

David J.A. Clines
November, 1978

Preface to the Second Edition

When it was decided at Sheffield Academic Press that it was time for yet another reprinting of this book, which I am pleased to know still fills a niche among textbooks on the Old Testament, I felt that this time there should be a second edition rather than a mere reprinting. But I soon came to feel that, though I was unhappy about some aspects of the book as it stood, I could not revise it from cover to cover, since that would make it an entirely different book. So I have compromised by editing the original book slightly, in particular removing the non-inclusive language, and by adding an Afterword, in which I try to register how the changes in my own thinking as a biblical scholar over the past two decades would have to be incorporated in the book should it ever be rewritten. I believe that the book in its present form still has a useful function for students, but now, twenty years after it was first conceived, I am the first to admit that it cannot be more than a first step, and that there are many new angles on the Pentateuch that deserve to be considered as well. I hope that with the aid of the Afterword readers will agree that the study of the theme of the Pentateuch is still in its infancy.

DJAC
May, 1996

1

Method

a. Negative

Two major tendencies in current Old Testament studies are challenged by the method and matter of this book; for that reason it will not be read with equanimity, and may well be discarded as superficial, by many of my colleagues in Old Testament research. I refer to the tendencies toward *atomism* and toward *geneticism*.

The tendency toward *atomism* is amply revealed by the contents pages of our learned journals. No one, for example, is surprised by the appearance of a ten-page article on a word that occurs only once in the Hebrew Bible. Then there is a literary form in scholarly literature known as the 'Note on ...' form: on Hosea 2.4a perhaps or even just on Hosea 2.4ab, since the author's contribution may concern only half a line of Hebrew poetry. Somewhere someone is interested in writing, and perhaps also in reading, articles on 'Apocryphal Cats' or 'Seating Arrangements at Divine Banquets in the Ancient Near East'. These are extreme examples, to be sure, of scholarly journal literature, and the type of research published in the journals should not perhaps be taken as representative of the overall direction of study within our field.

Nevertheless, the fact is that hitherto no Old Testament scholars, to my knowledge, have taken it upon themselves to write, except perhaps at a very popular level, an account of what they believe so large a tract of biblical literature as the Pentateuch is 'all about', or to express whether in the form of an article or a book their understanding of the theme or message or purpose or function (I use the terms loosely for the moment) of these first five books of the Bible. To be sure, it is a good sign that in recent decades attention has been drawn to issues of structure and theme in the larger units of the biblical writings. In the Pentateuchal field we have learned a great deal from the works of Hans Walter Wolff on 'The Kerygma of the Yahwist'[1] and 'The Elohistic Fragments in the Pentateuch',[2] from the study in the same vein on the Priestly Writers by Walter Brueggemann,[3] and from the volume on *The Yahwist: The Bible's First Theologian* by Peter F. Ellis.[4] But a yet more holistic approach to the Pentateuch is called for, which goes beyond questions about its (presumed) sources, and enquires about the meaning of the text that now exists.

The atomism of contemporary Biblical scholarship is founded ultimately on a scientific model of knowledge. This may be called the pyramid view of the accumulation of knowledge. Each worker is content to have made a little contribution (massive enough to himself or herself but trifling in proportion to the scale of the pyramid itself!), which with any luck will form part of a vast structure. Built upon the work of others, it will, its author hopes, be further built upon in its turn. Perhaps it will need adjustment or adaptation, sometimes it will be well-nigh hidden by a more elegant facing from another worker, and at times even the best stones have been known to be rejected by the builders. But the pyramid grows, and the workers on it find their own personal security and identity in their participation in the common enterprise.

Such a model of the accumulation of knowledge is an oversimplistic analysis of the growth of knowledge in the natural sciences, where a model of successive revolutions or of seismic shifts in the sets of presuppositions controlling the day-to-day activity of scientists might be more appropriate.[5] But, granting that the pyramid model is a rough approximation to what may be called 'normal' science, and that Old Testament study in some of its aspects (e.g. philology, archaeology) bears a certain resemblance to natural science, the model still gravely distorts the reality of our discipline. For our discipline belongs firmly in the tradition of humanistic studies, and inasmuch as it occupies itself with the interpretation of data that are already given, has more in common with the criticism of a body of well-known literature than with the discovery, accumulation and evaluation of new data. In the sphere of literary criticism knowledge does not accumulate steadily through the industry of objectively distanced scholars, but by means of repeated personal engagement with the text. When one learns from others, it is as much from the shaft of light the critic has brought to bear on the text, a total approach to the text, a setting of the text in a new context, that one learns, as from the detail of the commentator's explications. The model is that of the guide in a darkened museum who holds up a torch to reveal an unfamiliar object, or a familiar object from a fresh angle, in a new light.[6]

It is a mistake to believe that we can ever manage in biblical studies without both holistic and atomistic work. And it is only because caution, fear, or simple modesty has inclined so many scholars away from holistic approaches that I feel it necessary to defend an approach that ought to be self-evidently appropriate to the subject matter.

The second tendency, which it would be more exact to call an obsession, is toward *geneticism*.[7] By that I mean the study of the origins and development of the extant biblical text. It is no accident that the two most significant works in Pentateuchal studies in this century, Gerhard von Rad's *The Problem of the Hexateuch*[8] and Martin Noth's *A History of Pentateuchal Traditions*,[9] are both representative of this approach. Again a particular view of the nature of knowledge is implied by the genetic approach: it is that an object is best understood if its origins are uncovered, a text is best interpreted if its sources can be reconstructed and its pre-history determined. Now, such an approach may suit some subjects of study better than others. When, as in Old Testament studies, the sources and pre-history of our present texts are for the most part entirely hypothetical, and when, in any case, a work of art, such as a good deal of Old Testament literature undoubtedly is, yields its significance to the observer as a whole and through the articulation of its parts in its present form, one would have imagined that a genetic approach would not be strongly favoured. But it is, and it must indeed be confessed that many Old Testament scholars know of no other way of doing research on the Old Testament except along such lines. I do not decry such methodology; it is a scientific necessity, even if its firm results turn out to be meagre. But I do protest against the dominance of that approach, and set forth, by way of an alternative approach, the method adopted in this book as a gainful form of employment in Old Testament study.

Mine is not the first or only voice to be raised against the primacy of the genetic method. Some, like the structuralists, have silently opted out of geneticism. But some few, like Brevard Childs of Yale,[10] Luis Alonso Schökel of the Pontifical Biblical Institute in Rome,[11] or Walter Wink in his provocative little book, *The Bible in Human Transformation*,[12] have already given voice to their dissatisfaction with the genetic approach especially when attention has been diverted from the extant text. Gerhard von Rad, whose early work on the detection of two strands in the Priestly source of the Pentateuch would qualify him as an honoured member of the geneticists' club, knew where he stood at the end of the day, and stated categorically in his Genesis commentary apropos of chapters 2–3:

> Reconstruction of the original texts ... is not the primary task of exegesis ... No matter how much a knowledge of the previous stages of the present text can preserve us from false exposition, still there is no question that the narrative of chs. 2f., in spite of certain tensions and irregularities, is not a rubble heap of individual recensions, but is to be understood as a whole with a consistent train of thought. Above all else, the exegete must come to terms with this existing complex unity.[13]

With such allies, I would be well advised, I know, not to 'protest too much', but to get on with some account of how a holistic approach to the Pentateuch may be pursued. So to the second half of this statement of method.

b. Positive

What is fundamental to my method is to begin with the Pentateuch in its final form. I do not wish here to be side-tracked by delicate questions of what precisely its 'final form' is. Is it the most ancient, pre-Massoretic, somewhat variant, texts? The Massoretically defined text still slightly at odds with itself in its various families or codices? The consonantal text or the vocalized text? The text of the latest editor whom we may credit with authorial intentions, or the text left by the latest of late glossators who added the final marginal note that eventually made its way into the 'text'? No doubt if I were treating the 'theme' of Jeremiah—if there is such a thing—I should have to take very seriously the major structural and compositional differences between the Hebrew and the Greek texts. Fortunately no problem of that order exists for the Pentateuch, and the scale of the investigation undertaken here renders the minutiae I have mentioned above mostly invisible to the naked eye.[14] Real though these questions are, the ordinary reader must surely be non-existent and the critic rare who needs to take them into account in understanding the work as a whole. And as for the Pentateuch, I submit that its overall theme may as well be understood by a person who has never seen a printed Hebrew Pentateuch—which is the nearest most scholars get to its 'final form'—as by the most competent Hebraist or textual critic. There is *trahison des clercs* for you!

So much for the 'final form'. What about 'the Pentateuch'? I shall be discussing later whether a work so variegated and so evidently an amalgam of diverse materials as the Pentateuch could possibly be said to have a 'theme'. All I am concerned with here is to assert that it is legitimate to treat the Pentateuch as a single literary work. That is to say, I argue that the Pentateuch is not merely the sum of the first five books of the Bible, nor is it the Tetrateuch (Genesis–Numbers) plus Deuteronomy, nor is it the Hexateuch (Genesis–Joshua) minus Joshua, but an independent work in its own right. *When* it was first recognized as such I do not know, though for the present purpose I am prepared to go along with the majority of scholarly opinion and locate its definitive edition in the fifth century BCE. But the date of its origin is quite beside the main point of my argument. The fact is that the Pentateuch has been recognized as a literary entity by Jews, Samaritans, Christians and Muslims for somewhere between twelve hundred and twenty-five hundred years. It is for that reason, if for no other, appropriate to ask what the work is *about,* which is to say, more or less: What is its theme?

Since in treating of 'theme' I am moving into hotly disputed territory where literary critics, formalists, structuralists, oral traditionists and lexicographers have been having a field day, I must ask the reader's good will in allowing me, in Chapter 2, to stake out my own claim by explaining how I understand 'theme' and related terms. My usages are, I hope, not arbitrary, nor yet simply tailored to fit the material I am exploring. But neither are they meant, though stated somewhat categorically, to be definitive.

In Chapter 3, I move into examination of the Pentateuch itself by way of what I call 'indicators' of its theme. Not every literary work offers so many explicit indications of its theme. Often the critic must search high and low for pointers to the work's intention. But within the Pentateuch such pointers are strategically planted and thickly sown; even a wayfarer need not err therein, as the saying goes, though perchance a scribe (scholar) may. Perhaps this chapter will also have a heuristic value, softening up the reader to the notion that the Pentateuch may after all be a literary work with a theme. It also presents, for the more sceptical, my first set of data showing that the quest for theme is not a subjective exercise. 'Theme' is not whatever you like to make it, especially when the text itself makes so much obvious.

Encouraged by the way the 'indicators' in the Pentateuch all point in the same direction, I state in the brief Chapter 4 what

I shall argue to be the theme of the Pentateuch.

Chapter 5 follows up the statement of theme with the textual data relevant to the theme, that is, the data that state it, allude to it, recapitulate it. It is unnecessary for the reader to study the whole of this chapter in detail in order to appreciate the weight of the evidence; but on the other hand it is quite impossible to feel the weight of the evidence without having it presented more or less *in extenso*.

In Chapter 6 the focus of attention shifts from passages where the theme is more or less explicitly stated to a survey of the total content of the Pentateuch (from Genesis 12 onward) under the guiding light of the theme as it has been stated. I can only hope that the reader experiences some of the same sense of discovery as I did when I first read the Pentateuch with this particular theme in mind, continually surprised to find how much of the material fell into place, made sense, or was illuminated when viewed from this perspective.

Genesis 1–11 and its theme demands a separate chapter to itself (Chapter 7). Not only is its material temporally prior to the first statements of what is to be the theme of the rest of the Pentateuch, and therefore hardly capable of being subsumed under that theme, but also the tendency of Genesis 1–11 is apparently in a quite different direction from that of the remainder of the Pentateuch. It seems to me therefore necessary to give close attention to the theme of Genesis 1–11 in itself, and then to examine how these chapters are related to what follows. I readily concede that disproportionate space has apparently been allotted to these chapters within the overall structure of the present book; but I think that they do raise special problems, and there can be little doubt that they have generated a secondary literature quite comparable in bulk to that created by the rest of the Pentateuch put together.

Then, since others have concerned themselves in part with the question of a structure for the Pentateuch, or have pointed out what seems to them the absence of structure or theme for certain sections of the Pentateuch, I devote Chapter 8 to exploring divergences between my treatment of the Pentateuch and some studies previously concerned with questions of theme. In the first place my purpose is to clarify how my understanding of theme differs from that of G. von Rad and others, and in the second it is to show how a stretch of text previously thought to be uncoordinated can be understood, from the viewpoint of the suggested theme, as a meaningful whole.

Only in Chapter 9 do I engage with and in the genetic approach. Some, especially those who have no time for so-called 'critical' scholarship, will think it a pity that, having cast the devil out of the front door, I end by letting him in at the back. Those, on the other hand, who are wedded to the genetic approach, will skip lightly over what I believe to be the heart of my study, and fasten on the chapter that does things their way, discussing the possible origins and literary history of elements of the theme. Both kinds of readers will have read me wrong. My aim in that chapter is simply to show how the thesis of the book *may* be integrated with the still current documentary hypothesis of Pentateuchal origins. I am no devotee of the Graf–Wellhausen theory, and I suspect that many who stick with it do so only on the ground that they would rather have a theory, however bad, than no theory at all (though they would rarely put it in quite that way). I can foresee a completely new shape to the question of Pentateuchal origins emerging in the next decades, though I have my doubts that today's dissenters from Wellhausenism will find a large following. When the turmoil over Pentateuchal origins and history settles down again—if it ever does—Chapter 9 will have to be rewritten. But whatever form it takes will not affect the essential purpose of the book, which enquires about the Pentateuch that now is, however it came to be. Chapter 9 springs from the intellectual curiosity that drives us to go 'beyond what is written'. It is not a *concession* to geneticism, but an example of it and so implicitly an argument for it—in its proper place.

The final chapter, Chapter 10, on the function of the Pentateuchal theme, arises from the historical-critical method, which, like the genetic method, is quite unexceptionable—in its place; that is, provided it recognizes and respects its limitations. It is ironic, is it not, that the soundest historical-critical scholars, who will find talk of themes and structures 'subjective' in the extreme, will have no hesitation in expounding the significance of a (sometimes conjectural) document from a conjectural period for a hypothetical audience of which they have, even if they have defined the period correctly, only the most meagre knowledge, without any control over the all-important questions of how representative of and how acceptable to the community the given document was. Nevertheless, the precariousness of such undertakings is no reason for shying away from them, and we will no doubt go on reconstructing circles of meaning for our (usually undatable) Old Testament documents. In the case of the Pentateuch I would hazard that we are on middle ground, between the firm and the quagmire, in reconstructing its historical setting and function. Once again, therefore, if there is any chance of gaining insight into a dimly lit historical period, we shall probably think the risks involved in building hypothesis on fragile hypothesis worthwhile. In this case I too think it is not a foolish undertaking, but even so I have to recognize that Chapter 10 also may one day have to be written again, or perhaps be unwritten altogether. Again, however, that will not affect the thesis I seek to present in this book.

So much for what we may hazard to have been the historical function of the Pentateuchal theme. But now, since the Pentateuch is not only a literary work, but also a religious literary work, it would be in bad taste—to say no more—to ignore the contemporary religious function the Pentateuchal theme can have among those who read the Pentateuch as part of their 'Scripture', however precisely they understand the idea of Scripture and their own relation to that Scripture. And even those who read the Pentateuch merely as 'literature' will, if they are at all influenced by prevailing currents in literary studies, resent any relegation of a work of such force and imagination to the shelves of antiquaries, and demand discussion of the Pentateuchal theme as developing, or perhaps thwarting, the reader's consciousness of life or reality. For the sake of both these groups, who must include nearly everyone who is likely actually to *read* the Pentateuch, the second part of Chapter 10 offers a few suggestions on the religious or theological function of the Pentateuch as a book that now is, and not only once was.

Finally, as for the thesis of this book, which concerns the theme of the Pentateuch, it may be as well for me to reject in advance the criticism that it is simply 'subjective', for it rests upon firm data in the text. But I equally resist making a claim, as most biblical scholars do implicitly or explicitly, of being 'objective', since whether my thesis is judged right or wrong is to my mind a matter of *insight,* which I reckon is somewhere near 'subjective'. On one level, then, this is an essay about the Pentateuch; on another, it is a programme for work in biblical studies. It is both about matter and about method.

2

Definitions

Any conjunction of the words 'theme' and 'Pentateuch' naturally leads students of the Old Testament to think of the work of Martin Noth in his study, *A History of Pentateuchal Traditions.*[1] So I must make it clear that what I have in mind as 'theme' bears little relation to what Noth understood by that term. For him the 'themes' of the Pentateuch are complexes or units of traditional material or, more precisely, brief elements of a confessional statement about Israel's early history which were expanded by more extensive narrative material.[2] The five major 'themes' of the Pentateuch (guidance out of Egypt, guidance into the arable land, promise to the patriarchs, guidance in the wilderness, revelation at Sinai), which provided its outline, were in his view further filled out by minor 'themes' such as the plagues in Egypt or the Baal Peor episodes. Thus for Noth there was no such thing as *the* theme of the Pentateuch. For him, the various themes of the Pentateuch do not cohere in a unity; they do not even necessarily presuppose or depend upon one another.

I have no quarrel with Noth's terminology, which serves its purpose well enough, but I want to use 'theme' in reference to a literary work in quite a different way. I need to say something about the terminology in general, and then about how it applies to the Pentateuch.

a. In General

The theme of a narrative work may first be regarded as a conceptualization of its plot. A statement that is merely a compressed narrative, for example, 'The Pentateuch tells the story of humanity and especially of Israel from the creation to the death of Moses', is not a statement of theme, though it may be a statement of content.[3] If plot can correctly be defined as 'a narrative of events, the emphasis falling on causality',[4] theme may be regarded as plot with the emphasis on conceptualized meaning.[5] For example, the theme of a narrative work may be formulated as 'how power corrupts', or 'the impossibility of re-living the past', or 'the divergence between the plans of Yahweh and the plans of humans'.[6] In conceptualizing plot, theme tends to focus its significance and state its implications.

A second formulation of the concept of 'theme' may be borrowed from W.F. Thrall and A. Hibberd: theme is 'the central or dominating idea in a literary work ... the abstract concept which is made concrete through its representation in person, action, and image in the work'.[7] This definition need not, of course, be understood as implying that the 'idea' or 'abstract concept' has any existence prior to its realization in the work.

A third way of expressing what I understand by 'theme' is to say that it is a rationale of the content, structure and development of the work. I do not mean 'rationale' or 'development' to be taken in a genetic or historical sense, but in terms of the work itself in its final form. A statement of theme offers, in abbreviated form, an account of why the material of the work is there, and of why it is presented in the order and shape in which it is.

A fourth clarification of the concept of 'theme' may be reached by asking: What functions does a statement of theme serve? At first sight it may appear insensitive, not to say naive, to suppose that any extended or complex work of literary art can be reduced to some (usually banal) general statement. So it is necessary to stress that a quest for 'theme' is no reductionist undertaking, as if the work itself were a disposable packaging for the 'idea' that comes to realization in it. Rather, a statement of theme functions, first, as an orientation to the work; it makes a proposal about how best to approach the work. And since the hermeneutical circle of interaction between text and interpreter is constantly in process, orientation is not merely a desideratum for beginners; because the interpreter's perspective on the work is gradually re-formed by the work itself, orientation is a continuing process.[8] Secondly, a statement of theme functions as a warning or protest against large-scale misunderstanding of a work. Thirdly, a statement of theme can serve as evidence that the work is coherent or systematic, and not a randomly agglutinative assemblage of materials. Fourthly, a statement of theme is the first step in formulating the message of the work within its historical context or in setting up guidelines within which future readings or interpretations of the work in different historical contexts may be considered legitimate. That is to say, the statement of theme can serve an historical-critical purpose, of attempting to lay bare what the author intended to convey to his or her audience, or it can act as a control on interpretations of the text that treat it as a relatively autonomous work of art, with polyvalent significance.[9]

A fifth approach to a definition of 'theme' is by way of an attempt to distinguish it from similar terms: 'intention', 'motif', 'subject', and so on. 'Theme' is both narrower and broader than 'the intention of the author'. It is narrower in that it may express only one aspect of an author's intention. That intention may be, variously, to influence a particular historical situation (e.g. of controversy), or to meet a psychological need on the author's part, or even to make money or gain prestige. 'Theme' refers only to that aspect of the author's intention that is expressed in the shape and development of the literary work. But, on the other hand, 'theme' is broader than 'author's intention' in that it cannot always be stated adequately in terms of what the author had consciously in mind: on the one side authors do not necessarily formulate the theme of their work even to themselves (see further paragraph 4 below), and on the other, readers are under no constraint to make their statement of theme in terms of the author's intention (rather than in terms of the work), especially when, as in the case of biblical literature, they have no access to that intention apart from the work itself.[10]

Theme is *broader* than 'motif'[11] or 'topos',[12] or 'typical scene'[13] or 'narrative pattern'[14] or 'theme' in the sense used by Parry and Lord in their studies of Southslavic epic[15] and adopted by other students of techniques of oral composition. It relates to larger units than do these other terms. I am concerned with theme in the sense of the theme of the whole work; one could not speak of *the* motif or *the* typical scene of a work. Even a recurrent motif[16] does not necessarily constitute a theme. Theme and motif are entities 'of the same substance', however, for the theme of a certain pericope may become a motif of a larger work into which the pericope is incorporated.[17]

To discern the 'theme' of a work is a *more perceptive* undertaking than to discover its 'subject'. Statements both of theme and of subject may be answers to the question, What is the work *about?* But to identify its subject is merely to classify, while to discover its theme is to see 'the attitude, the opinion, the insight *about* the subject that is revealed through a particular handling of it',[18] that is, to *understand* the work more deeply than merely knowing its 'subject' requires. 'Theme' of course arises out of the subject, but because it is a matter for deeper perception its identification is more complex and involves more subjective considerations than does an enquiry about the 'subject'. In a literary work, unlike a scientific or technical work, theme is not usually explicit. However, in archaic or archaizing epic works, the theme or some prominent aspect of it is often stated explicitly at the beginning: one thinks of the first line of the *Iliad* or of the *Aeneid,* or of the first paragraph of *Paradise Lost.* I shall be arguing that the theme of the Pentateuch from Genesis 12 onward is made quite explicit, though to discern the overall theme of the Pentateuch requires a little subtlety.

Four further questions about 'theme' are relevant to the present study:

1. Can there be more than one theme in a literary work? Ultimately, I think not. When different, divergent, or contradictory themes emerge other than the theme the critic has first identified, one has to adapt one's statement of the theme to take account of them. There may indeed be different *levels* of abstrac-

tion on which theme is sought, identified, and articulated. Thus a theme that is expressed largely in terms of the plot of a narrative work may not be easily identifiable with a theme that is expressed in 'structuralist' terms, for example, according to the actantial model of A.J. Greimas.[19] Nevertheless, on whatever level theme is sought and according to whatever model of thematic analysis is being employed, unity of theme is a function of the unity of the literary work.[20] Of course, in the case of a work like the Pentateuch, which is self-evidently a composition from other works, the possibility exists that it has no unity and no unified theme. So a second question arises:

2. How can the existence of a given theme in a literary work be demonstrated? I would reply that there is no way of *demonstrating* a theme to everyone's satisfaction. The only formal criterion for establishing theme is: the best statement of the theme of a work is the statement that most adequately accounts for the content, structure and development of the work. To state the theme of a work is to say what it means that the work is as it is.

3. How can theme be discovered? I know of no technique for exposing an implicit theme apart from: trial and error. Since theme arises from the subject, is a conceptualization of plot, and is of the same substance as motif, the critic has an area within which to move already mapped out. All one can do then is to examine likely candidates. That is the method I propose following in the study of Genesis 1–11 in Chapter 7 below. In the case of a more explicit theme, which I believe the theme of the rest of the Pentateuch to be, the method can only be by observation of the data placed before one's eyes; Chapter 5 offers a collection of relevant data for the bulk of the Pentateuch.

4. One more preliminary question raises itself: Does our theme need to have been in the mind of the author? Not necessarily. 'Theme' is an item from the conceptual equipment of the literary critic, and not necessarily of the creative artist. If a function of enquiry about theme is orientation to the work, the author needs no orientation to his or her own work, and so the

author may not conceptualize its theme. If theme encapsulates the meaning of the work, the theme and the work are created together in the author's mind. It is the critic or reader, looking for a way into the work, for what makes this work the work it is and not another, and for what makes it hang together, who needs to think about theme. None of this is to say that authors cannot or do not perceive the theme of their works or that they are not in many cases far better able to state the theme of their works than any of their readers or critics. All I am arguing is that we do not need to assure ourselves that such and such a theme could have been present in the mind of an author or conceptualized by him or her before we allow the possibility that such and such is the theme of the work.

b. In Application to the Pentateuch

If it is granted that the foregoing observations have some validity in reference to literary works generally, two questions arise when we seek to apply them to the Pentateuch, that is, to enquire after '*the* theme of the Pentateuch'. The first question is whether the Pentateuch, which is manifestly a collection of the most diverse materials originating from vastly different periods and outlooks, and 'pressed to the ultimate limits of what is possible and what is readable', as von Rad says,[21] can be said in any reasonable sense to be a unity, and thus to have a theme. The second question is whether, even if it can be argued that in some sense the Pentateuch is a unity (in that, for example, the narrative of events is ordered chronologically, and not randomly), any *theme* could have been imposed upon the material or formed out of the material by the redactor who gave the Pentateuch its final shape; would such an editor not have been so constrained by his traditional materials, which presumably had divergent themes and tendencies of their own, that he would have had no freedom to mould them according to any dominating idea or plan he may have had?

To the first question it has to be replied that we can expect no *a priori* demonstration that a work as variegated as the Pentateuch has a single dominating theme; only if one becomes convinced that a proposal such as is made in this book does adequately take account of the bulk of the material and does provide evidence of the coherence of the work is one likely to accept that the final form of the text is a literary unity, in the sense of having a theme. It is instructive to observe, however, that even from an a *priori* standpoint, Noth was willing to raise the question 'whether the combination of the sources ... actually did not give rise to something new, which transcended the individual sources and their particular content and put them in a peculiar light ... and hence whether in the final analysis the whole has not become greater than merely the sum of its parts'.[22] Noth in fact rejected this option, since he regarded the production of the final form of the Pentateuch as an essentially mechanical process, which did not allow any significant re-shaping of the material.[23] Nevertheless, the possibility is still worth discussion, since minor alterations in the received material, to say nothing of juxtapositions of differing traditional material, can result in large-scale differences of emphasis, significance and direction. G. von Rad may also be numbered among those who have admitted the possibility of a theme in the Pentateuch, since he actually called for more research to be carried out on this topic: 'There has been much too little enquiry', he wrote on the first page of his commentary on Genesis, 'into what the Hexateuch is as a whole, what its basic theme really is, and therefore the exposition of Genesis has often been somewhat atomistic'.[24]

To the second question two responses, not mutually exclusive, can be made. First, the final redactor can, with minimal interference, re-shape the total impact of his material (the relevant case of the end of the Yahwist's work will be discussed below). Secondly, it is not necessary to posit that the shape of the final work was *intended* by the redactor. Remarkably, even Noth allowed for the possibility that the 'something new', which the Pentateuch as a whole may form, could have developed 'beyond the conscious intentions of the redactors' and that the combination of the sources may have resulted, 'perhaps unintentionally', in new narrative connections and theological insights.[25] So a claim that such and such is the theme of the Pentateuch is not necessarily a claim that the final redactor of the Pentateuch conceptualized the theme of the work in the terms we employ. I have already argued, it will be recalled, in the discussion of 'theme' in general, that the critic's statement of theme need not have been present in such terms in the mind of the author.

3

Indicators

The first indicator I find that directs us toward the theme of the Pentateuch is the point at which it concludes. Chronologically speaking, the Pentateuch's narrative runs from creation to the death of Moses. But why should it conclude with the death of Moses? That is not a natural resting point for a narrative of the fate of the patriarchal family that has become a nation and has been journeying toward Canaan. For at that point the tribes are left on the wrong side of the Jordan, and the occupation of the land, which is the goal of the journey, lies before them. Joshua is indeed briefly introduced (Deut. 34.9), but not here by way of assurance that the occupation of the land will take place (contrast 31.3, 23); he is simply the one whom Israel is to obey. And the text immediately turns its back upon Joshua in order to pronounce its final encomium upon Moses. So we are left at the end of the Pentateuch at a point of tension or expectation: the goal of the journey has not been reached, and Israel's leader, the dominant human figure since the beginning of Exodus, is dead. Israel's future is open-ended, even perhaps in jeopardy.

If we look now at the end of Genesis we find a similar state of affairs: the death of Joseph (50.26), surrounded by his children and at peace with his brothers, appears to be a point of repose that brings the patriarchal narratives to a peaceful resolution. Yet in the context of the previous verse, in which Joseph has assured the patriarchal family, 'God will visit you, and you shall carry up my bones from here' (50.25), the coffin in Egypt turns out to be nothing permanent, but serves, quite paradoxically, to direct the reader's vision toward the future.

The other books of the Pentateuch, also, have been concluded by notes that sustain an impression of movement and a looking toward the future. Exodus concludes (40.34-38) with the cloud covering the tent and the glory of Yahweh entering the tabernacle and taking up its abode there. 'The presence of God which once abode on Mount Sinai now dwells in the sanctuary and accompanies Israel on her way.'[1] For the tabernacle is precisely the symbol of the *moving* presence of God: 'Throughout all their journeys, whenever the cloud was taken up from over the tabernacle, the people of Israel would go onward ... Throughout all their journeys the cloud of Yahweh was upon the tabernacle by day, and fire was in it by night, in the sight of all the house of Israel' (40.36, 38). Although the end of Exodus finds Israel encamped, and so apparently settled, at Sinai, it points forward definitively to the journeying that lies ahead.

Leviticus and Numbers, in spite of the apparently static quality of much of their contents, nevertheless sustain, by their conclusions, this same impression of movement. Thus, while Leviticus has consisted of 'the commandments that Yahweh commanded Moses for the people of Israel *on Mount Sinai*' (27.34; cf. 26.46), Numbers moves the venue yet closer to the land, for its contents have been 'the commandments and the ordinances that Yahweh commanded by Moses to the people of Israel *in the plains of Moab by the Jordan at Jericho*' (36.13). It has, moreover, contained narratives of the movements, however circuitous, of the tribes toward the land. Deuteronomy, though set in the same locale as Numbers, that is, 'beyond Jordan in the wilderness' (1.1),[2] marks a progression upon Numbers in that it is essentially directed toward the future, as the statement of the 'statutes and ordinances that you shall be careful to do in the land' (12.1; cf. 6.1, 10; 7.1; 9.1; etc.).

So there is a progression, both temporal and local, throughout the Pentateuch, a progression that does not simply signify that in the course of the narrative one thing happens after another, or that people move from one place to another; it is a progression that is prepared and anticipated and that is purposive and not directionless.

3. Indicators

From where does this movement in the Pentateuch receive its impetus? There can be little doubt that the answer must be: the promise to the patriarchs, with its various elements, and in its various formulations. 'Like a scarlet thread the promise runs through the whole subsequent history of the patriarchs ... and keeps the story moving, a movement which reaches towards coming fulfilment full of expectation and hope.'[3] It should be remembered at this point that our enquiry is not at the moment an historical one; so the vast scholarly literature dealing with genetic questions and the differentiation of the promise materials conceptually and historically is irrelevant here.[4] For my purpose the patriarchal promise means, in the first place (quite literally), Gen. 12.1-3, and in the second place the repetitions and amplifications it receives throughout Genesis.

The elements of the patriarchal promise have been variously analysed. At least the following can be isolated: the promise of a son; the promise of descendants; the promise of God's presence; the promise of God's blessing; the promise of the covenant; the promise of new pasture; the promise of a cultivated land.[5] Although these promises may have differing historical origins, from the viewpoint of content they fall naturally into three groups: the promises of posterity, of a relationship with God, and of land. All three are present, though not to the same degree, in Gen. 12.1-3, and are found in various combinations elsewhere in Genesis.[6]

Having pointed now to the shape of the Pentateuch as a movement towards goals yet to be realized, and having located the impetus of that movement in the divine promise that initiates the patriarchal narratives, I can now make a suggestion concerning the theme of the Pentateuch and then sketch its outworking.

4

Statement

My proposal is this: *The theme of the Pentateuch is the partial fulfilment—which implies also the partial non-fulfilment—of the promise to or blessing of the patriarchs. The promise or blessing is both the divine initiative in a world where human initiatives always lead to disaster, and are an affirmation of the primal divine intentions for humanity.* The promise has three elements: posterity, divine–human relationship, and land. The posterity-element of the promise is dominant in Genesis 12–50, the relationship-element in Exodus and Leviticus, and the land-element in Numbers and Deuteronomy. The contrast *and* the similarity of the promises to what precedes the patriarchal history are to be developed in Chapter 7 below, on Genesis 1–11.

5

Formulations

A demonstration of the theme of the Pentateuch as the fulfilment (or partial fulfilment) of the patriarchal promise is not very difficult. For the text itself articulates the promise in varying and repeated formulations, and often makes quite explicit attachments between narrative material and the divine promise that has brought the narrated event into being. Nevertheless, a great deal of the Pentateuchal material is related only implicitly to the promise in its various forms; how close that implicit relationship is will be treated in the next Chapter (6, Exposition).

I speak here of the patriarchal *promise*—in the singular—though its threefoldness is as important to my analysis as its oneness. For the triple elements are unintelligible one without the other, never strongly differentiated one from another in their manifestation in the text, and each, in the accumulative effect, with the implication of the others. Thus, what can a promise of Yahweh to a patriarch be if not a promise of a divine–human relationship? Yet what value can such a promise have to a Hebrew patriarch if it does not include his posterity? And what kind of a posterity can a patriarch envisage that does not dwell together in its own land?

Or if we take as our starting point a different element of the promise, the same theo(logical) nexus presses itself upon us: 'Go to the land that I will show you', says God in Gen. 12.1. What kind of land can it be that will replace 'your land' (*'arṣĕkâ*), the land of Abram's family and father's house, except a land that will become his land and the land of his family-to-be, the land where he himself will become head of a father's house? And what kind of a movement can it be from 'your land' to 'the land that I will show you' except one that presupposes Abram's obedience to the command and Yahweh's commitment to guidance of Abram, that is, one that implies a divine-human relationship?

Or of we take another starting point, the promise of heirs, as in Gen. 15.5, a promise of land immediately attaches itself to it almost inevitably, and we are compelled to ask: What can such a promise be but Yahweh's gift to Abram, the establishment of a contractual relationship between God and the patriarch (15.7, 9-21)?

Nonetheless, all the implicates of the promise are not spelled out on each occasion when it is made, reiterated, or alluded to. And especially because the elements of the promise are fulfilled—in so far as they *are* fulfilled—sequentially throughout the Pentateuch, in the order descendants–relationship–land, I present in this chapter the textual evidence for the character and quantity of the promise material. Only the simplest analysis—into the three 'elements' of the promise—has been made, so that the reader may appreciate the extent of these elements and the areas where they are most densely concentrated. The promise itself, in its various forms, is of course found chiefly in Genesis and the opening chapters of Exodus. Specific allusions to the promise, however, continue throughout the Pentateuch, intensifying in Deuteronomy to such a degree that full quotation of them becomes otiose, and mere citation of the chapter and verse references must eventually suffice.

The first three sections (a–c) of this chapter, then, present the texts containing statements of the promise according to each of its three constituent elements; the fourth section (d) presents allusions to the promise, whether to the promise as a whole or to one of its elements.

a. The Promise of Descendants

Genesis

12.2 I will make you into a great nation.
12.7 to your seed (I will give this land).
13.15 (all the land that you see I will give to you and) to your seed for ever. And I will make your seed like the dust of

	the earth, so that if one can count the dust of the earth, your seed also will be able to be counted.
15.4f.	One who will come forth from your loins will be your heir ... Look toward heaven and count the stars, if you are able to number them ... So will your seed be.
15.13, 16	Your seed shall be a sojourner in a land that is not theirs ... four hundred years.
15.18	To your seed (have I given this land).
16.10	[The angel of Yahweh to Hagar] I will greatly multiply your seed, and it will not be able to be numbered for multitude.
17.2	(I will make my covenant between me and you, and) I will multiply you exceedingly.
17.4-7	You shall be the father of a multitude of nations ... Your name will be Abraham, for I have made you the father of a multitude of nations ... (And I will establish my covenant between me and you and) your seed after you throughout their generations (to be a God unto you and unto) your seed after you.
17.16	I will bless her [Sarah], and also I have given you a son from her; I will bless her, and she shall be a mother of nations; kings of peoples shall come from her.
17.19f.	Sarah your wife shall bear you a son ... I will establish my covenant with him for an everlasting covenant for his seed after him. And as for Ishmael ..., behold, I have blessed him, and I will make him fruitful and multiply him exceedingly; twelve princes shall he beget, and I will make him a great nation.
21.12f.	Through Isaac shall your seed be named. And also the son of the bondwoman I will make into a nation, because he is your seed.
21.18	[The angel of Yahweh to Hagar] (Arise, lift up the lad) ... for I will make him into a great nation.
22.16ff.	By myself I have sworn ... that I will indeed bless you, and I will multiply your seed as the stars of the heaven, and as the sand that is upon the sea shore. And your seed (shall possess the gate of its enemies), and by your seed shall all nations of the earth bless themselves (*hitbārăkû*).
26.3f.	[to Isaac] To you and to your descendants (I will give all these lands) ... I will multiply your seed as the stars of heaven, and (I will give to) your seed (all these lands); and by your seed all the nations of the earth shall bless themselves (*hitbārăkû*).

26.24 [to Isaac] I will multiply your seed for the sake of Abraham my servant (cf. 26.28-29).

28.13f. [to Jacob] (The land on which you lie, to you I will give it) and to your seed. And your seed will be like the dust of the earth, and you shall spread abroad to the west and to the east, to the north and to the south. And by you and your seed all clans of the earth will bless themselves (*nibrĕkû*).

35.11-12 [to Jacob] Be fruitful and multiply; a nation and a congregation of nations shall be from you, and kings shall come out of your loins; (and the land I gave to Abraham and to Isaac to you I will give it) and to your seed after you (I will give the land).

46.3 [to Jacob] Do not fear to go down to Egypt, for there I will make you into a great nation.

b. The Promise of Relationship

Genesis

12.2f. (I will make you into a great nation) and I will bless you (sing.) and make your name great; and be a blessing! And I will bless them who bless you and him who curses you I will curse, and by you all clans of the earth will bless themselves (or, be blessed) (*nibrĕkû*).

17.1-11 I am El Shaddai; walk before me, and be blameless. And I will make my covenant between me and you (and will multiply you exceedingly) ... Behold, my covenant is with you, and you shall be the father of a multitude of nations. And your name will no longer be Abram, but your name will be Abraham; for I have made you the father of a multitude of nations ... And I will establish my covenant between me and you and your seed after you throughout their generations, to be a God unto you and unto your seed after you ... and I will be their God ... And as for you, you shall keep my covenant, you and your seed after you ... This is my covenant, which you shall keep ... Every male among you shall be circumcised ... and it shall be a token of a covenant between me and you.

17.16 I will bless her [Sarah], and also I have given you a son from her; I will bless her, and she shall be a mother of nations.

17.17ff. I will establish my covenant with him [Isaac] for an everlasting covenant for his seed after him. And as for Ishmael ..., behold, I have blessed him, and will make him fruitful ... But my covenant I will establish with Isaac.

26.2f. [to Isaac] Do not go down to Egypt. Sojourn in this land, and I will be with you, and will bless you.

26.24 I am the God of Abraham your father; fear not, for I am with you and will bless you.

28.13, 15 [to Jacob] I am Yahweh, the God of Abraham your father and the God of Isaac ... And behold, I am with you and I will keep you wherever you go, and I will bring you back to this land; for I will not leave you until I have done what I have spoken to you.

35.9f. God appeared to Jacob again ... and blessed him. And God said to him, Your name is Jacob; no longer shall your name be called Jacob, but Israel shall be your name.

46.3 [to Jacob] I am God, the God of your father; do not be afraid to go down to Egypt ... I will go down with you to Egypt, and I will also bring you up again.

48.21 [Jacob to Joseph] God will be with you, and will bring you again to the land of your fathers.

Exodus

3.6 [to Moses] I am the God of your father, the God of Abraham, the God of Isaac, and the God of Jacob.

3.12 I will be with you; and this shall be the sign for you that I have sent you: when you have brought forth the people out of Egypt, you shall serve God upon this mountain.

3.15f. Yahweh, the God of your fathers, the God of Abraham, the God of Isaac, and the God of Jacob (*bis*).

4.5 Yahweh, the God of their fathers, the God of Abraham, the God of Isaac, and the God of Jacob.

4.23 Let my son go, that he may serve me in the wilderness.

5.1 Let my people go that they may hold a feast to me.

6.6ff. Say to the people, I am Yahweh ... and I will take you to me for a people, and I will be to you a God; and you shall know that I am Yahweh your God who is bringing you out from under the burdens of Egypt.

7.16 Let my people go, that they may serve me (in the wilderness) (also 8.1 [Heb. 7.26]; 8.20 [Heb. 16]; 9.1, 13; 10.3).

Leviticus

26.12 I will walk among you, and I will be to you a God, and you shall be to me a people.

Included within the comprehensive category of 'relationship' are several kinds of formulation of the relationship between God and the patriarchs or the nation. That is to say, sometimes the relationship is expressed as a blessing, sometimes as a 'being with' or guidance, sometimes as a continuance of God's relationship with former patriarchs. Though some scholars conceive of these formulations as independent elements within the promise, they can be conveniently grouped as a category of 'relationship', distinct from, though often combined with, the promises of land and descendants.

The promise of *blessing* is, as Rendtorff has noted,[1] sometimes found outside, and introductory to, the promise itself (thus Gen. 35.9-11; 48.3-4), and sometimes within the promise (thus 12.2; 26.3; 28.4). Most commonly, the promise of blessing is linked with the promise of descendants (17.16, 20; 22.17; 26.24; 28.3), as Westermann pointed out;[2] but there is no special significance in this fact, since 'blessing' is also conjoined with 'being with' and possession of the land (26.3) or simply with the land (28.4). It is not surprising that in Genesis, with its preoccupation with the continuation of the patriarchal line, blessing should be most frequently linked with the promise of descendants.

The promise of *being with* (Gen. 26.3, 24; 28.15; 31.3; cf. 31.5; 35.3; and 31.42; 48.21) is likewise a promise of relationship. Sometimes it appears in connection with movement ('I am with you and will keep you wherever you go', 28.15), but elsewhere in a context of settlement ('Sojourn in this land, and I will be with you', 26.3 [cf. 31.5]). So it is inappropriate to subsume this promise under that of 'guidance'.[3]

The promise of *guidance* is a specific application of the promise of 'being with'. No fixed formula is used, but it is evident, for example, in 46.4, 'I will go down with you to Egypt, and I will also bring you up again', and in 28.15, 'I am with you and will keep you wherever you go'.

Expressions about the *continuance of God's relationship* with the former patriarchs, such as 'the God of your father' (e.g. Gen. 46.3) or 'the God of your fathers' (e.g. Exod. 3.15), also function within the category of the relationship element of the promise. For the assurance that the God who speaks is the God who has pledged himself to one's father and his descendants is a reassurance of the hearer's own relationship to God. At the same time, the appearance or speech of a God who styles himself 'the God of the father(s)' functions as a *fulfilment* of the promise of relationship. Such self-predications, or references to God under such a title, could equally well appear under section (d) below: 'Allusions to the promise'.

c. The Promise of Land

Genesis

12.1	Go from your country ... to the land that I will show you.
12.7	To your descendants I will give this land.
13.14-15	Lift up your eyes and look from the place where you are, to the north and to the south, and to the east and to the west; for all the land that you see I will give to you and to your seed for ever.
13.17	Arise, walk through the land in its length and breadth, for to you I will give it.
15.7	(I am Yahweh who brought you out of Ur of the Chaldees) to give you this land to inherit.
15.13, 16	(Your seed will be a sojourner in) a land that is not theirs ... (but in the fourth generation) they will come back hither.
15.18	To your seed I have given this land, from the river of Egypt to the great river, the river Euphrates, (that is, the land of) the Kenite, the Kadmonite, the Hittite, the Perizzite, the Rephaim, the Amorite, the Canaanite, the Girgashite, and the Jebusite.
17.8	I will give to you, and to your seed after you, the land of your sojournings, all the land of Canaan.
22.17	Your seed shall possess the gate of its enemies.
26.2ff.	[to Isaac] Dwell in the land of which I shall tell you ... To you and to your seed I will give all these lands ... I will give to your seed all these lands.
28.13, 15	[to Jacob] The land on which you lie, to you I will give it and to your seed ... (Behold, I am with you, and I will keep you wherever you go, and) I will bring you back to this land.
35.12	The land that I gave to Abraham and Isaac I will give to you, and to your seed after you I will give the land.

46.3f. [to Jacob] Do not be afraid to go down to Egypt ... I will go down with you to Egypt, and I will also bring you up again.

Exodus

3.8 [to Moses] And I have come down to deliver them [my people] from the hand of the Egyptians, and to bring them up out of that land into a good and large land, unto a land flowing with milk and honey, to the place of the Canaanite, the Hittite, the Amorite, the Perizzite, the Hivite, and the Jebusite.

3.17 I have promised (*'āmar*): I will bring you up out of the affliction of Egypt into the land of the Canaanite, the Hittite, the Amorite, the Perizzite, the Hivite, and the Jebusite, to a land flowing with milk and honey.

6.6ff. Say to your people, I am Yahweh ..., Yahweh your God, who is bringing you out from under the burdens of Egypt; and I will bring you into the land concerning which I lifted up my hand to give it to Abraham, to Isaac, and to Jacob; and I will give it to you for a heritage.

23.23-33 When my angel goes before you and brings you in to the Amorite, the Hittite, the Perizzite, the Canaanite, the Hivite, and the Jebusite ... none shall be barren in your land ... Little by little I will drive them out from before you, until you have increased, and inherit the land. And I will make your border from the Reed Sea to the Sea of the Philistines, and from the wilderness to the River [Euphrates]; for I will deliver the inhabitants of the land into your hand, and you shall drive them out ... They will not dwell in your land.

34.24 I will dispossess nations from before you, and I will enlarge your border; and no one shall covet your land when you go up to appear before Yahweh your God three times in the year.

d. Allusions to the Promise

Genesis

18.19f. I have chosen him [Abraham] that he may charge his children and his household after him to keep the way of Yahweh by doing righteousness and justice, so that Yahweh may bring upon Abraham what he has spoken (*dibbēr*) of him.

21.1 And Yahweh remembered Sarah as he had said (*'āmar*) and Yahweh did to Sarah as he had spoken (*dibbēr*).

24.7 Yahweh ... who promised (*dibbēr*) me and swore to me: To your seed I will give this land.

24.60 [to Rebekah] Our sister, be the mother of thousands of ten thousands! And may your seed possess the gate of their enemies!

26.3 [to Isaac] To you and your seed I will give all these lands, and I will fulfil the oath that I swore to Abraham your father.

28.3f. [Isaac to Jacob] May El Shaddai bless you and make you fruitful, so that you may become a company of peoples. May he give the blessing of Abraham to you and to your seed with you, that you may take possession of the land of your sojournings, which God gave to Abraham.

28.13ff. [to Jacob] I am Yahweh, the God of Abraham your father and the God of Isaac; the land on which you lie, to you I will give it and to your seed. And your seed will be like the dust of the earth, and you shall spread abroad to the west and to the east, to the north and to the south. And by you and by your seed all clans of the earth will bless themselves (*nibrĕkû*). And behold, I am with you, and I will keep you wherever you go, and I will bring you back to this land; for I will not leave you until I have done what I have spoken (*dibbēr*) to you.

31.5 The God of my father has been with me.

31.42 If the God of my father, the God of Abraham and the Fear of Isaac, had not been on my side ...

32.9, 12 (Heb. 10, 13) O God of my father Abraham and God of my father Isaac, O Yahweh who did say to me, Return to your country and to your kindred, and I will do you good ... You did say, I will do you good, and make your seed like the sand of the sea, which cannot be numbered for multitude.

35.3 The God who ... has been with me wherever I have gone.

35.12 [to Jacob] The land that I gave to Abraham and Isaac I will give to you, and to your seed after you I will give the land.

47.27 Israel dwelt in the land of Goshen, and gained possessions in it, and was fruitful and multiplied exceedingly.

48.3f. [Jacob to Joseph] El Shaddai ... appeared to me and blessed me, and said to me, Behold, I will make you fruitful, and multiply you, and I will make of you a company of peoples, and I will give this land to your seed after you for an everlasting possession.

48.15f. [Jacob] The God before whom my fathers Abraham and Isaac walked, the God who has shepherded me all my life long till this day, the angel who has redeemed me from all evil, bless the lads [Ephraim and Manasseh]; and in them may my name be perpetuated and the name of my fathers Abraham and Isaac; and may they grow into a multitude in the midst of the earth.

48.21 I am about to die, but God will be with you, and will bring you again to the land of your fathers.

50.24 [Joseph to his brothers] God will assuredly visit you and will bring you up from this land to the land that he swore to Abraham, to Isaac and to Jacob.

Exodus

1.7 And the sons of Israel were fruitful, and increased abundantly, and multiplied, and waxed exceedingly mighty, and the land was filled with them.

1.9f. [The pharaoh] The people of the sons of Israel are more numerous and mighty than we. Come, let us deal shrewdly with them, lest they multiply.

1.12 The more they were oppressed, the more they multiplied and the more they spread abroad.

1.20 God dealt well with the midwives, and the people multiplied and grew very strong.

2.24 And God heard their groaning, and God remembered his covenant with Abraham, with Isaac, and with Jacob.

6.4f. And also I established my covenant with them [Abraham, Isaac, and Jacob] to give them the land of Canaan, the land of their sojournings in which they sojourned ... and I have remembered my covenant.

6.8 I will bring you into the land concerning which I lifted up my hand to give it to Abraham, to Isaac, and to Jacob.

13.5 When Yahweh brings you into the land ..., which he swore to your fathers to give to you ...

13.11 When Yahweh brings you into the land of the Canaanite, as he swore to you and to your fathers that he would give it to you ...

32.10, 13 [to Moses] I will consume them and I will make you into a great nation ... [Moses to Yahweh] Remember Abraham, Isaac and Israel, your servants, to whom you did swear by your own self, and did promise (*dibbēr*) unto them, I will multiply your seed as the stars of the heavens; and all this land that I have spoken of (*'āmar*) I will give to your seed and they will inherit it for ever.

33.1, 3 [to Moses] Go ... you and the people ... to the land that I swore to Abraham, to Isaac and to Jacob, saying, To your seed I will give it ... unto a land flowing with milk and honey.

5. Formulations

Leviticus

14.13 [to Moses and Aaron] When you come into the land of Canaan … which I am giving to you for a possession …

18.3 [to Israel] You shall not do as they do in the land of Canaan, to which I am bringing you.

19.23 When you come into the land and plant all kinds of trees, for fruit …

19.33 When a stranger sojourns with you in your land …

20.22 You shall keep all my statutes … so that the land, to which I am bringing you to dwell, may not vomit you out.

20.24 I have said to you, You shall inherit their land, and I will give it to you to possess, a land flowing with milk and honey.

23.10 When you come into the land that I am giving you …

23.22 When you reap the harvest of your land …

25.2 When you come into the land that I am giving you …

26.4f. (If they confess their iniquity) I will remember my covenant with Jacob, and also my covenant with Abraham I will remember, (and the land I will remember).

26.44f. (When they are in the land of their enemies, I will not reject them) to break my covenant with them, for I am Yahweh their God; but I will remember for their sake the covenant with their forefathers (whom I brought forth from the land of Egypt in the sight of the nations) that I might be their God; I am Yahweh.

Numbers

10.29 [Moses to Hobab] We are setting out for the place of which Yahweh said, I will give it to you. Come with us, and we will do you good, for Yahweh has promised *(dibbēr)* good concerning Israel.

13.1 [to Moses] Send men to spy out the land of Canaan, which I am giving to the people of Israel.

14.7f. [Joshua] The land, which we passed through to spy it out, is an exceedingly good land. If Yahweh delights in us, he will bring us into this land, and will give it to us, a land that flows with milk and honey.

14.12 [to Moses] I will strike them with the plague and disinherit them, and I will make you into a nation greater and mightier than they.

14.16 [Moses imagines Egyptians saying] Because Yahweh was not able to bring this people into the land that he swore to them, he has slain them in the wilderness.

14.22ff. None of the men who have seen my glory and my signs … shall see the land that I swore to their fathers … But my servant Caleb ... I will bring into the land into which he went, and his seed shall possess it.

14.30f. No one shall come into the land where I swore that I would make you dwell, except Caleb ... and Joshua. But your little ones ... I will bring in and they shall know the land that you have despised.

14.40, 42f. [Israel] See, we are here; we will go up to the place that Yahweh said (*'āmar*) ... [Moses] Do not go up, for Yahweh will not be with you.

15.2 When you come into the land of your habitations, which I am giving to you ...

15.18 When you come to the land to which I am bringing you ...

15.40 ... so that you may be holy to Yahweh your God. I am Yahweh your God, who brought you out of the land of Egypt to be a God to you; I am Yahweh your God.

16.12ff. [Dathan and Abiram to Moses] You have not brought us into a land flowing with milk and honey, and you have not given us an inheritance of fields and vineyards.

16.41 (Heb. 17.6) [Israel to Moses and Aaron] You have killed the people of Yahweh.

16.45 (Heb. 17.10) [Yahweh to Moses] Get up from among this congregation, so that I may consume them in a moment.

17.27f. (Heb. 17.12f.) [Israel to Moses] Behold, we perish, we are undone, we are all of us undone ... Are we all to perish?

18.20 [to Aaron] You shall have no inheritance in their land, and no portion of land shall be yours among them ...

20.4 [Israel to Moses] Why have you brought the congregation of Yahweh into this wilderness, to die here?

20.12 [to Moses and Aaron] Because you did not believe in me, to recognize me as holy in the sight of the Israelites, you shall not bring this congregation to the land that I have given them.

20.24 (Aaron) shall not enter the land that I have given to the Israelites, because you rebelled against my word ...

21.5 [Israel to God and Moses] Why have you brought us up out of Egypt to die in the wilderness?

21.24 Israel smote him [Sihon] with the edge of the sword, and took possession of his land from the Arnon to the Jabbok.

21.31 Then Israel dwelt in the land of the Ammonites.

21.35 And they smote him [Sihon] and they took possession of his land.

22.12 [God to Balaaml You shall not curse the people, for it is blessed.

23.8 [Balaam] How shall I curse whom God has not cursed?

	How can I execrate whom God has not execrated?
23.10	[Balaaml Who has counted the dust of Jacob or numbered the dust-clouds (?) of Israel?
23.20f.	[Balaam] He [Yahweh] has blessed, and I cannot revoke it ... Yahweh his [Israel's] God is with him.
24.9	[Balaam] Blessed be those who bless you, and cursed be those who curse you.
25.18	[Balaam] And Edom shall become a possession and Seir, his enemies, shall become a possession.
26.53	To these shall the land be apportioned as an inheritance.
32.5, 32f.	[The Gadites and the Reubenites to Moses] Let this land [Jazer and Gilead] be given to your servants for a possession ... We will pass over armed in the sight of Yahweh into the land of Canaan, and the possession of your inheritance shall remain with us beyond Jordan. And Moses gave to them ... the kingdom of Sihon ... and the kingdom of Og ... the land round about.
33.5f.	[Yahweh to Moses for Israel] When you cross over the Jordan into the land of Canaan, then you shall drive out all the inhabitants.
33.54	You shall inherit the land by lot according to your families.
34.2	When you enter the land of Canaan, this shall be the land that will fall to you for an inheritance: the land of Canaan with its territories ...
34. 13	This is the land that you shall inherit by lot ...
34.17	These are the names of the men who shall divide the land to you for an inheritance ...

Deuteronomy

1.8	[Moses] Behold, I have set the land before you; go in and possess the land that Yahweh swore to your fathers, to Abraham, to Isaac, and to Jacob to give to them and to their seed after them.
1.10f.	Yahweh your God has multiplied you, and behold, you are this day as the stars of the heaven. May Yahweh, the God of your fathers, make you a thousand times as many as you are, and bless you, as he has promised (*dibbēr*) you.
1.20f.	[at Kadesh-barnea] I said to you, You have come to the hill-country of the Amorites, which Yahweh your God is giving to us. See, Yahweh your God has set the land before you; go up, take possession, as Yahweh, the God of your fathers, has promised (*dibbēr*) you.
1.25	[the spies] It is a good land that Yahweh your God is giving to us.

1.35f. Not one of these men ... shall see the good land, which I swore to give to your forefathers, except Caleb ... To him and to his children I will give the land on which he has trodden.

1.39 Your little ones ... and your children ... shall go in thither, and to them I will give it, and they will possess it.

2.7 Yahweh your God has blessed you in all the work of your hand ... these forty years Yahweh your God has been with you.

2.12 (Esau's descendants dispossessed the Horites) as Israel did to the land of its possession, which Yahweh gave them.

2.24 I have given into your hand Sihon ... and his land; begin to possess it!

2.29 ... until I go over the Jordan into the land that Yahweh our God gives to us.

2.31 Yahweh said ..., Behold, I have begun to deliver up Sihon and his land before you; begin to possess it!

4.20 Yahweh has taken you ... out of Egypt, to be a people of his own possession.

4.31 (When Israel is in exile) Yahweh your God ... will not fail you or destroy you or forget the covenant with your fathers, which he swore to them.

4.37 Because he loved your fathers and chose their descendants ... to bring you in, to give you their land for an inheritance ...

5.3 Not with your fathers did Yahweh make this covenant [of Horeb], but with us, who are all of us alive this day.

5.31 (Heb. 5.28) [to Moses] Stand by me, and I will speak unto you all the commandment, and the statutes, and the ordinances, which you shall teach them, that they may do them in the land that I am giving them to possess (cf. 6.1).

6.3 Hear, Israel, and observe to do [the commandment] that it may be well with you, and that you may increase greatly as Yahweh the God of your fathers has promised (*dibbēr*) to you, [in] a land flowing with milk and honey.

6.10 When Yahweh your God brings you into the land that he swore to your fathers, to Abraham, to Isaac, and to Jacob, to give to you ...

6.18f. You shall do what is right and good in the sight of Yahweh, that it my be well with you, and that you may go in and take possession of the good land that Yahweh swore to give to your fathers by thrusting out all your enemies from before you, as Yahweh has promised (*dibbēr*).

6.23 ... that he might bring us in and give us the land that he swore to give to your fathers.

7.8 It is because Yahweh loves you, and is keeping the oath that he swore to your fathers, that Yahweh has brought you out ...

7.12f. Yahweh your God will keep with you the covenant and the loyalty that he swore to your fathers, and he will love you, bless you, and multiply you ... in the land that he swore to your fathers to give you.

8.1 All the commandments ... you shall observe to do, that you may live and multiply, and go in and possess the land that Yahweh swore to give to your fathers.

8.18 You shall remember Yahweh your God, for it is he who gives you power to get wealth; that he may establish the covenant that he swore to your fathers.

9.5 ... because of the wickedness of these nations Yahweh your God is driving them out from before you, and so that he might establish the word that Yahweh swore to your fathers, to Abraham, to Isaac, and to Jacob.

9.26-29 I prayed to Yahweh, O my Lord Yahweh, do not destroy your people and your heritage ... Remember your servants, Abraham, Isaac, and Jacob ... lest the land [of the Egyptians] say, Because Yahweh was not able to bring them into the land that he promised (*dibbēr*) them and because he hated them, he has brought them out to slay them in the wilderness. For they are your people, and your heritage ...

10.11 Arise, go on your journey ... that they may go and possess the land that I swore to their fathers to give to them.

10.15 Yahweh set his heart in love upon your fathers and he chose their seed after them.

10.22 Your fathers went down to Egypt with seventy persons; and now Yahweh your God has made you as the stars of heaven for multitude.

11.9 ... that you may prolong your days upon the land that Yahweh swore to your fathers to give to them and to their seed, a land flowing with milk and honey.

11.21 ... that your days and the days of your children may be multiplied in the land that Yahweh swore to your fathers to give them.

13.17 ... that the Lord may multiply you, as he swore to your fathers.

15.4 Yahweh will bless you in the land that Yahweh your God gives you for an inheritance to possess.

15.6 Yahweh your God will bless you, as he promised (*dibbēr*) you.

19.8 If Yahweh your God enlarges your border, as he has sworn to your fathers, and gives you all the land that he promised (*dibbēr*) to give to your fathers ...

26.3 [at firstfruits, an Israelite will say to the priest] I declare this day to Yahweh your God that I have come into the land that Yahweh swore to our fathers to give us.

26.5 A wandering Aramaean was my father, and he went down into Egypt ... few in number; and there he became a nation, great, mighty and populous ... and [Yahweh] brought us into this place and gave us this land, a land flowing with milk and honey.

26.15 Bless your people Israel, and the ground that you have given us, as you swore to our fathers, a land flowing with milk and honey.

26.18f. Yahweh has declared today concerning you that you are a people for his own possession, as he promised (*dibbēr*) you, and that you are to keep all his commandments ... that you shall be a people holy to Yahweh your God, as he has promised (*dibbēr*).

27.3 ... when you pass over to enter the land that Yahweh your God gives you, a land flowing with milk and honey, as Yahweh, the God of your fathers, has promised (*dibbēr*) you ...

27.9 [Moses and the Levitical priests to Israel] This day you have become the people of Yahweh your God.

28.9ff. Yahweh will establish you as a people holy to himself, as he has sworn to you, if you keep the commandments of Yahweh your God ... And all the peoples of the earth shall see that you are called by the name of your God ... and Yahweh will make you abound in the fruit of your body ... in the land that Yahweh swore to your fathers to give you.

28.62 [If Israel disobeys] Whereas you were as the stars of heaven for multitude, you shall be left few in number.

29.10-13 (Heb. 29.9-12) You stand today, all of you, before Yahweh your God ... so that you may enter into the covenant and oath of Yahweh your God, which Yahweh your God is making with you today, so that he may establish you today for himself as a people, and that he may be God to you, as he promised (*dibbēr*) you and as he swore to your fathers, to Abraham, to Isaac, and to Jacob.

30.16 [if you obey the commandments[4]] then you shall live and multiply, and Yahweh your God will bless you in the land that you are entering to take possession of.

30.20 ... loving Yahweh your God ... that you may dwell in the

	land that Yahweh swore to your fathers, to Abraham, to Isaac, and to Jacob, to give them.
31.7	... the land that Yahweh has sworn to their fathers to give them.
31.20f.	When I have brought them into the land flowing with milk and honey, which I swore to their fathers ... the land that I swore to give.
31.23	[to Joshua] You shall bring the children of Israel into the land that I swore to give them; I will be with you.
34.4	[to Moses] This is the land that I swore to Abraham, to Isaac and to Jacob, saying, I will give it to your seed.

Other references to the land (or, gates, cities, etc.) that Yahweh has given (or, is giving): Deut. 3.2, 18, 20; 4.1, 21, 40; 5.16, 31 (Heb. 28); 6.10, 23; 9.6, 23; 11.17, 31; 12.1, 9 (cf. 10); 13.12 (Heb. 13); 15.4, 7; 16.5, 18, 20; 17.2, 14; 18.9; 19.1; 2, 10, 14; 20.16; 21.1, 23; 24.4; 25.15, 19; 26.1, 2; 27.2, 3; 28.8, 52; 32.49, 52.

Other references to Yahweh as the 'God of the fathers' who is giving the land: Deut. 4.1; 6.3; 12.1.

Other references to entering and/or taking possession of the land: Deut. 4.5, 14, 22; 26; 5.33 (Heb. 30); 6.1, 18; 7.1; 8.7; 9.5; 11.8, 10, 11, 29, 31; 12.29; 19.14; 21.1; 23.20 (Heb. 21); 28.21, 63; 30.5, 16, 18; 31.13; 32.47.

Other references to dispossessing nations: Deut. 9.1; 11.23; 12.2, 29; 18.12, 14; 19.1; 31.3.

Other references to crossing Jordan (viz. to take possession of the land): Deut. 9.1; 12.10; 27.2, 4, 12; 30.18; 31.2, 13; 32.47.

6

Exposition

a. Genesis

If we may leave aside for consideration in the next chapter the 'Primaeval History' (Genesis 1–11) and concentrate our attention here on the remainder of the book (chs. 12–50), it is immediately apparent that this major section of Genesis concerns the fortunes of four individuals: Abraham, Isaac, Jacob and Joseph. These four figures are not, however, presented as individuals, but as a line of succession. In thematic terms, Genesis 12–50 is primarily concerned with the fulfilment (or, perhaps, the non-fulfilment) of the posterity-element in the divine promises to the patriarchs.[1] The theme appears at first in the shape of questions: first, will there be even one son, let alone a posterity?; and secondly, once the son is born, will he survive to produce a posterity (note especially ch. 22)? In this question about the fulfilment or otherwise of the promise lies the significance of the triple narrative of the 'ancestress in danger' (chs. 12; 20; 26), the significance of the barrenness of the wives of the patriarchs (Sarah, Rebekah, Rachel), the significance of the fraternal rivalries that endanger the life of one or more of the heirs of the promise (Ishmael;[2] Jacob; Joseph; Benjamin), and the significance of the famines in the land of Canaan (Gen. 12.10; 26.1; 41.54) that threaten the survival of the patriarchal family as a whole. An intricate pattern of selections, threats, separations, and contentions forms the bulk of the Genesis material,[3] preventing the rapid growth of the Abrahamic family, but never negating the fulfilment of the promise.

And what has happened to the promise by the end of the book? In 46.27 we read, 'All the persons of the house of Jacob, who came into Egypt, were seventy'—which means that the family has become established, and, barring drastic misfortunes, is likely to survive, but that the vision of descendants as many as the stars of heaven (15.5) or the sand of the sea (22.17), and of Abraham as father of a multitude of nations (17.5), has yet to be realized. To be sure, in Egypt the sons of Israel are fruitful and multiply exceedingly (47.27), but even so Jacob still must pray on his deathbed that his grandsons Ephraim and Manasseh will 'grow into a multitude' (48.16), and it is only within Exodus that the multiplication of the patriarchal family attains significant dimensions (Exod. 1.7, 9, 12, 20). Genesis ends with the patriarchal family consisting essentially of Jacob and his twelve sons. The promise has begun to take effect, but is still largely unrealized.

The thematic elements of the land and of the divine relationship also appear in Genesis, but in a subsidiary role. The land that is to be 'given' to the Abrahamic family (e.g. 12.7) is indeed 'shown' to Abraham, and explored (e.g. 12.5-9; 13.17) and lived in by the patriarchs, but it remains the property of the Canaanites ('the Canaanite was then in the land' [12.61 serves as backdrop for the whole of Gen. 12–50]) except for one burial plot (23.17-20), and a piece of land for the building of an altar (33.1, 9f.). In a way, the events of ch. 12 turn out to be symbolic of—if not programmatic for!—the relationship of the patriarchs to the land. Here Abram arrives in the land (12.5), only to walk, so to speak, straight through it and out the other side (12.10)! All that Abram has met with in the land that Yahweh would 'show' (12.1) him is 'the Canaanite' and 'a famine' (12.6, 10), while the only word he has received from Yahweh is a promise, 'Unto your seed I will give this land' (12.7)—which is not very encouraging for Abram personally. True, things improve in ch. 13, but on the whole the patriarchal narratives take place outside the promised land almost as much as inside it, the possession of the land remains a hope (28.4), and while the descendants of Abraham to whom the land is not promised (cf. 35.12) have 'their dwelling places in the land of their possession' (36.43), the heirs of the promise of the land find themselves, at the end of the book, firmly outside the land and settled in Egypt. The promise has been repeatedly affirmed, but except in the slightest degree it remains no more than a promise.

As for the promise of the divine relationship, its formulation in Genesis remains somewhat cryptic and its outworking variable and provisional. In 12.3 it is in terms of blessing, whether of Israel or of the nations or of both,[4] and in terms of a patronage that operates against Israel's enemies as well as for its allies (cf. also 27.29). In ch. 17 it is a covenant, which, although it is linked with reiterated promises of progeny (17.2, 4ff.), is essentially a 'covenant to be God to you and to your descendants' (17.7). Yet what the covenant will entail beyond the practice of circumcision, which is properly only the 'sign' of the covenant (15.11), is undisclosed. Elsewhere the relationship is expressed as a 'being with' (26.3, 28; 28.15, 20; 31.5; 35.3; 39.2, 21), which results in 'blessing' or protection; and God has become the God of the father(s) of the patriarch (e.g. 28.13; 31.5, 42; 32.9). In brief, within Genesis it is by no means established in set terms what the nature of the divine–human relationship is to be. The promise has begun to take effect, but the shape it will adopt is as yet uncertain.

b. Exodus and Leviticus

It is in these books that the element in the promise of God's relationship with the descendants of Abraham is most clearly brought to expression. At the two focal points of these books, the exodus event and the Sinai revelation, it becomes plain what the promise meant by its words, 'I will bless you', 'I will make my covenant between me and you', 'I will be your God'.

Thus in the book of *Exodus* the narrative of the exodus from Egypt is *initiated* by acts that spring from the divine–human relationship: God remembers his covenant with the patriarchs (2.24), while Moses' commissioning comes from the God of the fathers (3.6) who will be 'with' Moses to bring forth 'my people' in order to 'serve' God upon the mountain (3.10ff.). Likewise in ch. 6 the deliverance from Egypt will be an expression of the divine relationship: 'I appeared to Abraham, to Isaac and to Jacob; I will deliver you, and I will take you for my people, and I will be your God; and you shall know that I am Yahweh your God, who has brought you out ...' (6.3, 6f.). Characteristically, throughout the confrontation with the pharaoh Israel begins to be described by Yahweh as 'my people' (7.4, 16; 8.1; cf. 3.10; 4.22), whose future is to lie in their relationship of 'service' to Yahweh: 'Let my people go, that they may serve me' (7.16; 8.1, 20; 9.1; etc.). And Yahweh begins to describe himself as 'God of the Hebrews' (7.16; 9.1; 10.3; cf. 5.3). In short, the whole series of negotiations between Moses and the pharaoh (chs. 5–11) concerns permission for the Hebrews to formalize their relationship with their God by 'serving' him cultically with sacrificial offerings. Of what precise nature the offerings are to be they do not know; Moses announces, as if programatically for Leviticus: 'Our cattle must go with us ... for we must take of them to serve Yahweh our God, and we do not know with what we must serve Yahweh until we arrive there' (10.26).[5]

The *exodus narrative proper* opens with a command-speech of Yahweh (12.2-20), which is followed by an act of worship (12.27) and a three-fold obedience formula (12.28; 12.35; cf. 11.12; 12.50). Already it is being established by such speech forms and responses what the relationship of Yahweh and his people is to be. The narrative continues with a guidance motif (13.17f., 21f.; 14.2), again suggestive of the command–obedience relationship. As for the deliverance at the Sea, the relationship is of Yahweh as warrior and Israel as the feeble protégé who has 'only to be still' (14.13f., 25). With the utmost brevity and insight, the poem of ch. 15 signifies that what has happened in the exodus event is the fulfilment of the promise 'I will be your God': 'this is my God, and I will praise him, my father's God, and I will exalt him' (15.2). This second thematic element, that of the relationship, is already fulfilled at the exodus, but still remains to be more fully realized.

As for the *transitional material* between the Reed Sea and Sinai (15.22–19.2), it does not provide merely a temporal or a geographical link, but in fact an important thematic element. For here the promise of relationship is called in question. Yahweh has taken Israel as his people, but it is now opened up to doubt whether, for its part, Israel intends to take Yahweh as its God. The 'murmurings' of Israel are, as Moses says, 'not against us but against Yahweh' (16.8). Israel questions whether Yahweh is 'among us or not' (17.7). Yahweh's responses are acts of self-demonstration: when the quails and manna come, 'then you shall know that I am Yahweh your God' (16.12); and when the Israelites ask, 'Is Yahweh among us or not?' (17.7), the victorious outcome of the battle with Amalek (17.8-16) answers the question. By way of contrast to Israel's hesitancy in accepting Yahweh as their God, ch. 18 presents a whole-hearted acceptance of Yahweh by the non-Israelite, Jethro: when he hears of 'all that God had done for Moses and for Israel his people' (18.1) he confesses, 'Now I know that Yahweh is greater than all gods' (18.11), and he offers sacrifice (18.12). (A similar pattern has developed in Genesis: once the promise of progeny has begun to be fulfilled by the birth of Isaac, the promise is called in question by the threat to his life in ch. 22. We shall meet the same kind of tension again in a moment, with the Sinai narrative.)

Once *Sinai* is reached, the first divine speech focuses on this very matter of the relationship between God and Israel: 'You shall be my own possession among all peoples' (19.5), it begins. Even though all the earth is Yahweh's, Israel is his in a way that other nations are not: 'a kingdom of priests and a holy nation' (19.6). Characteristically, the first commandment expresses the relationship in the most basic terms: 'I am Yahweh your God' (20.2). Other forms of expression of the relationship abound in the Sinai narrative: it is a meeting with God (19.17), a talking with Israel by God (20.22), a seeing of God (24.10), and a sharing in a communal meal with God (24.11). The relationship also appears in the form of words of command followed by an obedience formula: 'obey my voice' (19.5) followed by 'All that

Yahweh has spoken we will do' (19.8). Such a pattern frames the whole of the tabernacle instructions (25.1, etc.; cf. 35.1, 4, 29; 39.42f.), and a similar pattern frames the 'covenant code': 'these are the ordinances that you shall set before them' (21.1), concluded by 'All the words that Yahweh has spoken we will do' (24.3). The relationship is further expressed by the offering of sacrifice (24.5f.; cf. 20.24f.) and the ratification by sacrifice of the covenant enshrined in the 'book' (24.7f.) or upon the tables of stone (34.27f.).

As if to highlight that what is happening at Sinai is primarily the establishment of the relationship of God and Israel (which is a fulfilment of the divine promise), in the middle of the Sinai narrative is located an episode that threatens to *destroy* the relationship. The threat is of the creation of anti-gods who claim Israel's allegiance: 'These are your gods, O Israel, who brought you up out of the land of Egypt' (32.4). Rejection of this element of the promise (the relationship) immediately puts the rest of the promise into jeopardy, for Yahweh's reaction is to say: 'I will consume them; but of you [Moses] I will make a great nation' (32.11). Moses responds by invoking the patriarchal promise of progeny and land (32.13), and the threat is averted. But for the moment it has looked as if the relationship is going to be rescinded bilaterally. Thereafter the debate of ch. 33 revolves around the question of what kind of a relationship there can be, now that it has been strained almost to breaking point.[6] Will Yahweh himself now go up to the land with Israel? (no [33.3; cf. 32.34]; an angel will take his place); will Yahweh's presence go with Moses? (no [33.14]; Moses shakes off the promise that insists on attaching itself to him alone, and demands that the response include the people[7]). The debate is resolved only in Yahweh's concession (v. 17) to Moses' demand that it be a relationship that is a 'going with us, so that we are distinct, I and thy people, from all other people who are on the face of tile earth' (v. 16; cf. 34.9).

Thus we have seen in Exodus a large-scale elaboration of the element of relationship in the patriarchal promise; between the two foci of the narrative (exodus and Sinai) and also within the latter focus there have intervened challenges to the promise (the 'murmurings'; the golden calf). These challenges have temporarily put the promise under threat, but have issued in closer definition of the nature of the relationship.

As for the book of *Leviticus*, its *function*, within the scheme of the promise and its fulfilments, is to spell out in detail the means by which the relationship now established is to be maintained. The regulation of ritual worship is its almost exclusive interest: its presuppositions are that humans will wish to offer gifts to God, will sin against God, will want to know the will of God for everyday life. That is to say, Leviticus depicts a community exploring its relationship with God.

The *form* of Leviticus corresponds to its function as an elaboration of the relationship of Israel with God: the majority of its sections are represented as a speech of command to Moses and Israel (e.g. 1.1; 4.1; 6.1 [Heb. 5.20]; 8.1), which is sometimes explicitly concluded by an obedience formula (e.g. 8.36: 'Aaron and his sons did all the things that Yahweh commanded by Moses'; cf. 16.34). Even when the response of Israel is not made explicit, it is perfectly clear that the relationship is to be one of command and obedience.

The *nature* of the material in Leviticus as an expression of the divine–human relationship is properly described in the book's concluding summaries: 'These are the statutes and ordinances and laws that Yahweh made between him and the people of Israel on Mount Sinai by Moses' (26.46; cf. 27.34). And the intention of Leviticus as a guide for the preservation of the divine–human relationship is clearly spelled out in its peroration: 'If you walk in my statutes and observe my commandments and do them ... I will walk among you, and will be your God, and you shall be my people. I am Yahweh your God' (26.3, 12f.).

Do then the fulfilments of the promise of a divine–human relationship that occur in these books mean that this aspect of the promise is now completely fulfilled? No, for the promise of a relationship is not a contract that can be signed and sealed, and thereupon stored away in the vaults of the past. A relationship contains a dynamic for development; it constantly remains open. So at the exodus and at Sinai something is set in train rather than accomplished. The exodus has been only a going out, and thus a beginning, and the words of God from Sinai point not to the present but to the future with their 'You *shall* ... you *shall* not'. Even Leviticus, apparently static and timeless law, is to be understood as 'in fact not directed to the past but to the present and future'.[8] The fact that modes of relationship still exist means the possibility of reconstruction even for a community that seems bent on destroying itself. Both Exodus and Leviticus therefore lead into a future in which Israel has yet to discover what this promise of a relationship, 'I will be your God and you shall be my people', will mean.

The other elements in the promise play a minor role in Exodus and Leviticus. The promise of a *progeny* that becomes a great nation forms an important motif in the first chapter of Exodus (1.7, 9, 10, 12, 20), but thereafter the promise is only implicitly alluded to in the dangers that threaten it: the command of the pharaoh to exterminate male Israelite children (1.22), the possibilities of death in the wilderness (14.11f.; 16.3; 17.3), the fearfulness of too close an approach to the holy mountain (19.21) or to the direct address of God (20.19), and the divine determination to destroy the people after the incident of the golden calf (32.9). It is only this last threat, with the proposal to substitute Moses for Abraham, that calls forth an explicit restatement of the promise; Moses says, 'Remember Abraham, Isaac, and Israel, your servants, to whom you swore by your own self, and said to them, "I will multiply your descendants as the stars of heaven"' (32.13). Immediately Yahweh is reminded of the promise, the threat vanishes: 'Yahweh repented of the evil that he thought to do to his people' (32.14). It will only be in the event of persistent disregard of God's chastisements that the promise will be called into question in the future (Lev. 26.38), and even then the repentance of a remnant will cause Yahweh to remember his covenant with Jacob, Isaac and Abraham (26.42) and he will not 'abhor them [the remnant] so as to destroy them utterly and break my covenant with them' (26.44). But even here it is striking that the promise of progeny is subordinated to the promise of the relationship, which is the primary theme of these two books: Yahweh will 'remember the covenant with their forefathers, whom I brought forth out of the land of Egypt in the sight of the nations, that I might be their God' (26.45). And certainly Israel has not yet become a 'great nation'; the promise of progeny awaits a fuller realization,

The promise of the *land,* though more prominent, nevertheless appears only in scattered allusions throughout Exodus and Leviticus, compared with the dominant role it will assume in Numbers and Deuteronomy. The promise given to Moses by the God of the fathers is that 'I will bring you up out of the affliction of Egypt, to the land of the Canaanites ..., a land flowing with milk and honey' (3.17), while the covenant made with the patriarchs is expressed in ch. 6 in terms of the gift of the land of Canaan (6.4, 8). At crucial moments in the narrative of Exodus the land is held out, however briefly, as the goal of Yahweh's activity: at the institution of the Passover (13.5, 11), at the crossing of the Sea (15.13, 17), at the giving of the manna (16.35), at the conclusion of the Covenant Code (23.23, 31), at the episode of the golden calf (32.13), at the command to depart from Sinai (33.1, 3). Leviticus for its part recognizes that some of its laws can take effect only after Israel has entered the land; so in this book the land is held out not as the goal of the ongoing activity, but at most as the context for performing the law of Yahweh. The land forms the context for the law of the leprous house (14.34), for the law regarding fruit-trees (19.23), for the law of first-fruits (23.10), for the fallow-year law (25.2), Above all, the land is the context in which Israel will realize its holy distinctiveness from the nations of the earth: 'You shall not do as they do in the land of Egypt, where you dwelt, and you shall not do as they do in the land of Canaan, to which I am bringing you. You shall not walk in their statutes. You shall do my ordinances and keep my statutes and walk in them. I am Yahweh your God' (18.3f.). And certainly the land still lies a long way ahead: by the end of Leviticus Israel has yet to leave Mt Sinai. So it is not the land that is the central element of the promise in Leviticus!

c. Numbers and Deuteronomy

In these books the aspect of the patriarchal promise most in evidence is that of the *land*. Their orientation and movement is towards the land, the promise of which is—by the end of these books—partly and proleptically fulfilled, but to a large extent unfulfilled.

In *Numbers* the idea of movement toward the land appears at the very beginning of the book in the census of the people (ch. 1). Though hints have previously been given of a conception of the Israelite tribes as a military community (they go up from Egypt 'equipped for battle' [Exod. 13.18] and they are brought out 'in their hosts' (*ṣābāʾ*) [Exod. 6.26; 7.4; etc.[9]]), it becomes very plain at the beginning of Numbers that what is being portrayed are the first preparations for a military occupation of the land; for what takes place is a census of all males 'from twenty years old and upward, all in Israel who are able to go forth to war' (1.3). It is understood from the beginning that the land that is promised will nonetheless have to be fought for. The Levites are not included in this census (1.47-53) because they will not be involved in the fighting; their census will be on a different principle: of the Levites, 'every male from a month old and upward you shall number' (3.15). What will be significant about the total of Levites is how it corresponds to the first-born of the rest of Israel who are reckoned as Yahweh's possession and must be 'redeemed' (3.40–51). Hard upon the census of ch. 1 comes the rules for the disposition of the camp (ch. 2); they clearly presuppose the ongoing movement of the people towards the land (2.17). Even the chapters concerning the position and duties of the Levites (chs. 3–4) concern them *vis-à-vis* the moving camp (cf. e.g. 4.5). There follows a variety of laws that have little in common (lepers, 5.1-4; marital 'jealousy', 5.11-31; the Nazirite, 6.1-21), but they all concern the purity of the camp and the people and are no doubt inserted here, as de Vaulx observes, 'in order to show that the people will only be able to depart for the conquest of the promised land if it is in a state of sufficient purity and generosity'.[10] Even the chapters (7–9) that record gifts made for the tabernacle, the cleansing of the Levites, and the observance of passover begin and end on notes that keep the matter of movement towards the land in the forefront of attention. The first gifts made for the tabernacle are of wagons and oxen (7.1-8), the means of its transportation; and on the day when the tabernacle is finally established and the cloud covers it (9.15f.), an elaborate account is proleptically introduced to depict how the cloud functions during the movement of the camp: 'Whenever the cloud was taken up from over the tent, after that the people of Israel set out; and in the place where the cloud settled down there the people of Israel encamped' (9.17; cf. 18-23). The final item of tabernacle-related furniture is, significantly again, the silver trumpets (10.1-10), which will serve as signals for breaking camp (10.2, 6). The author 'moves naturally from the cloud as a signal for the departure of the Israelites to the other signal to them to assemble and move off, the silver trumpets'.[11]

Throughout this first third of Numbers, though the materials are very diverse, and not generally recognized to follow any organizing principle, there runs this strong emphasis on the function of these last commands from Sinai for the journey toward the land. Leviticus has, with a few exceptions we have noted above, largely envisaged a cult that could be carried out anywhere—even in the wilderness—indefinitely. Numbers, by contrast, even in these early chapters (1.1–10.10), cannot be thought of as a mere appendage to the revelation from Sinai; movement away from Sinai towards the land accounts for almost all its material.

At Num. 10.11 the movement actually begins: 'the cloud was taken up from over the tabernacle of the testimony, and the people of Israel set out by stages from the wilderness of Sinai' (10.11f.); the departure is not a voyage into the void, but expressly, as Moses says to Hobab, a 'setting out for the place of which Yahweh said, "I will give it to you"' (10.29). The patriarchal promise is thus recalled, the departure notice is recapitulated (10.33), and within the space of a couple of chapters Israel is poised on the brink of Canaan, while the spies are sent out and actually enter the land (ch. 13). Embryonically the promise of the land has now begun to be fulfilled. The intervening chapters (11–12) function as a question mark about progress toward the land:[12] not only is there a craving for food like the fish that the Israelites ate in Egypt (11.4, 13), a backward-looking desire that leads to the destruction of some of the people (11.33f.), but also there is rebellion against Moses (ch. 12)—as well as a feared rebellion against Moses (11.26-29)—who alone is the mediator of the divine guidance to the land; for Israel sets out on the journey 'at the command of Yahweh by Moses' (10.13) and the movement of the ark is accompanied by Moses' ritual word (10.35f.).

Just as we have seen in both Genesis and Exodus, no sooner does the promise begin to come into effect than it is beset by questions and negations. Thus between the departure from Sinai and the arrival at the borders of Canaan there are incidents that threaten the promise; the very act of token entry by the spies into the land is effectively negated by their majority report that the land is 'a land that devours its inhabitants' (13.32)—how much less can it support Israel as well![13] And the ensuing chapter relates the most grave threat of all to the promise of the land: at the very brink of entry to the land, Israel decides to 'choose a captain, and go back to Egypt' (14.4). It is as if Israel is willing the promise to fail, and must destroy Moses as the man through whom alone the promise can be effected (14.10). Not for the first time (cf. Exod. 32.10) Yahweh is minded to destroy Israel and start afresh with Moses (Num. 14.12), but once again it is Moses' appeal to the patriarchal promise (14.16; cf. Exod. 32.13) that halts the divine wrath; Yahweh can compromise by decreeing that none of the present generation except Joshua and Caleb 'shall see the land that I swore to give to their fathers' (14.23, 30f.). And still the ensuing narrative revolves around the question of whether Israel will enter the land: when in a fit of repentance they determine to 'go up to the place that Yahweh has promised' (14.40), they are soundly defeated by Amalekites and Canaanites (14.45). Before movement toward the land begins again, a catena of motifs previously used appears again: there is cultic legislation pertinent to the time 'when you come into the land you are to inhabit, which I give you' (15.2), 'when you come into the land to which I bring you' (15.18); there is renewed questioning of the authority of Moses (ch. 16), accompanied in part perhaps by a refusal by Dathan and Abiram to 'go up' into the land (16.12, 14)[14] and a perverse application of the conventional description of Canaan as 'a land flowing with milk and honey' to *Egypt* (16.13)—which is to call in question the land of promise as a goal; there is finally the fear, constantly recurring throughout the wilderness material, of death—here (17.12f.) it is the matter of the danger of proximity to the divine presence, which is resolved by the appointment of the Levites as guardians of the sanctuary (chs. 18–19).

The land comes back into focus as the goal in ch. 20, where Israel sets out for the land, albeit by a circuitous route. While Moses and Aaron now learn that they themselves will not enter the land (20.12, 24) and while the possibility of death in the wilderness, before the land is ever reached, keeps recurring (20.4; 21.5), the land is still being held out before the people as Yahweh's gift to them (20.4, 24). By ch. 21 Israel has begun, for the first time, to take possession of land (Sihon's, 21.24f.; Og's, 21.35). The land Israel acquires is not yet regarded as *the* land, but the possessing of *this* land is a kind of warming-up process for the taking of *the* land that is the goal of these books. At the beginning of the next chapter (ch. 22) it seems that the goal has been attained: Israel finds itself 'in the plains of Moab beyond the Jordan at Jericho' (22.1), the final jumping-off point for the entry of the land. But, frustratingly, it is the very same point where Israel will still be standing at the end of Numbers (36.13) and presumably also of Deuteronomy (34.8). For the second time now the land has come within sight but the promise of possession remains unfulfilled.

Immediately upon Israel's arrival at the threshold of

fulfilment of the promise, there occur, within the Balaam story (chs. 22–24), echoes of the elements of the original promises to Abraham: none can 'count the dust of Jacob' (23.10; cf. Gen. 13.16; 15.5); 'Yahweh their God is with them' (23.21); 'Blessed be every one who blesses you, and cursed be every one who curses you' (24.9; cf. 23.8, 20; cf. Gen. 12.3). Yet the land still lies in the future, and even then it is not the land of Canaan but only the land of Edom that the seer envisages as Israel's possession ('Edom shall be dispossessed', 24.18). From that high point, where the promises appear to be on the brink of fulfilment, we descend to ch. 25, where Israel 'yokes' itself to Baal of Peor (25.3), and 'bows down' to the gods of Moab (25.2), so calling into question the promise of Yahweh's exclusive relation with Israel. But the sequel to the Baal Peor episode, in which there has been purged from Israel those who have rejected exclusive allegiance to Yahweh, is a renewed census of the people—in the plains of Moab by the Jordan at Jericho (26.3)—with an eye to the occupation of the land. As in 1.3, it is a census of 'all in Israel who are able to go forth to war' (26.2), for the movement forward into the land has not been forgotten. That census accomplished, the division of the land is commanded (26.53-56)—before the Jordan has ever been crossed!; and problems of inheritance of parcels of land are ironed out (27.1-11)—before any land has actually been possessed!

Finally, when the Midianite/Moabite threat to the promise has been eliminated by vengeance on the Midianites (ch. 31), the occupation of land begins in earnest: the 'land that Yahweh smote before the congregation of Israel' is 'given to [his] servants for a possession' (32.4f.). Two and a half tribes enter upon 'the possession of [their] inheritance' (32.32), so that the promise of land has now been partly fulfilled, though it is still of course largely unfulfilled. To signal the fact that the goal is now in sight, we are invited in ch. 33 to review the stages of Israel's journey from Egypt via many places of no significance to that place of vast significance, which is geographically the terminus of the Pentateuch: the plains of Moab by the Jordan at Jericho (33.48).

Its significance, of course, lies, not in itself, but in what it foretokens and allows: the possession of Canaan. There follow instructions for the time 'when you pass over the Jordan into the land of Canaan' (33.51), concerning the treatment of the Canaanites and the method of distribution of the land (33.50-56); then (34.1-15), a demarcation of the boundaries of the land, 'the land of Canaan in its full extent' (34.2 RSV), the names of the men 'who shall divide the land to you for inheritance' (34.16-29), the possessions of the Levites (35.1-8), the cities of refuge (35.9-28), the problem of pollution of the land by blood (35.29-34), the question of the inheritance of the daughters of Zelophehad (36.1-12). Nothing is here, in short, in these last five chapters of the book, but what concerns the *land.*

As far as *Deuteronomy* is concerned, it goes without saying that everything focuses upon the land. Among its most characteristic phrases are 'the land you are to possess', which occurs (with variations) 22 times, and 'the land (*or,* ground, gates, cities, etc.) that Yahweh your (*or,* our, etc.) God gives you (*or,* us)', which occurs 34 times.[15] The speeches of Moses of which it largely consists are set 'beyond the Jordan' (1.1, 5; cf. 9.1; 31.2), 'in the land of Moab' (1.5; 29.1), the place of proleptic significance. The first speech (1.5–3.29) recounts the movement of Israel from Horeb toward the land under the impulse of the patriarchal promise now renewed: 'Behold, I have set the land before you; go in and take possession of the land that Yahweh swore to your fathers, to Abraham, to Isaac, and to Jacob, to give to them and to their descendants after them' (1.8). The hortatory appendage to the first speech (4.1-40) begins and ends with reference to the land: 'Give heed to the statutes and the ordinances that I teach you ... that you may live, and go in and take possession of the land that Yahweh, the God of your fathers, gives you' (4.1); 'You shall keep his statutes and his commandments ... that you may prolong your days in the land that Yahweh your God gives you for ever' (4.40). The second speech (5.1–26.19) again begins with Sinai (5.2-33), this time with concentration on the words from Yahweh rather than on the events of the journey. Already at

Sinai it is made clear that the commandments look toward the entry into the land: to Moses God says, 'Stand here by me, and I will tell you all the commandments ... that you shall teach them, that they may do them in the land that I give them to possess' (5.31; cf. 6.1; 12.1). Constantly the land is 'the land that Yahweh has promised (*dibbēr*)' (6.3, 19; 9.28), the land sworn to the fathers (6.10, 18, 23; 7.8; 8.1; 10.11); possession of the land will confirm the covenant and the word sworn to the fathers (8.18; 9.5). Deuteronomy, therefore, is oriented to the land that yet remains to be entered, and regards the entry into the land as essentially a fulfilment of the patriarchal promises. In no part of the Pentateuch is the thesis better sustained that the theme of the Pentateuch is the partial and yet awaited fulfilment of the patriarchal promise.

Even in Deuteronomy, however, sight is not lost of the other elements of the divine promise. The *land* that is held out before Israel as the goal of its journey from Sinai (1.8) is a land to be inhabited by the numerous progeny of which the promise had spoken. Already at Sinai, Moses says, the promise of descendants has been fulfilled: 'Yahweh your God has multiplied you, and behold, you are today as the stars of the heaven for multitude' (1.9; cf. 10.22 and Gen. 15.5f.; 22.17). But in the same breath Moses denies that the promise has been exhausted: it has not yet been completely fulfilled, for he goes on to say, 'May Yahweh, the God of your fathers, make you a thousand times as many as you are, and bless you, as he has promised (*dibbēr*) you' (1.11). The promise to the patriarchs is expressly referred to, and its scope is understood as continually broadening. Israel has already become a 'great nation' (4.6ff.; cf. 26.5), but it has not ceased to grow: 'you will beget children and children's children' (4.25). The commandments Israel receives through Moses will apply to a continuing succession of generations (5.3; 6.2; 7.9; 29.28), who will need to be reminded of those fulfilments of the promise that have already been accomplished (6.20-23). Yet fulfilment is always a matter of degree and the 'great nation' (4.6), as many as the stars (1.9), is, from another perspective, 'the least of all peoples' (7.7), confronted by nations greater than itself (7.17; 11.23).

As for the promise of a divine–human *relationship,* in Deuteronomy there appear many markers to show both that it is fixedly established, and in what terms it exists. In brief, Deuteronomy's most common locution, 'Yahweh your (*or,* our) God',[16] occurring more than 300 times, reiterates the permanency of the relationship, while the constant reference to 'commandments', 'statutes', 'judgments' (singly or in combination) along with exhortations to 'love' God (11 times), and references to the 'covenant' (23 times) designate the character of the relationship. The major speech of Moses concludes on this note: 'Yahweh has declared concerning you today that you are to be a people for his own possession, as he has promised (*dibbēr*) you, and that you are to keep all his commandments, and that he will set you on high above all nations that he has made, in praise and in fame and in honour, and that you should be a people holy to Yahweh your God, as he has promised (*dibbēr*)' (26.18f.). Israel's relationship to Yahweh as a commandment-keeping people, holy to Yahweh, has already come about, in conformity with the promise, and has yet to be more completely fulfilled, in conformity with the promise. Deuteronomy envisages also the possibility of Israel's abandonment of the relationship: before it has been set curse as well as blessing, the attraction of other gods as well as loyalty to Yahweh (11.26ff.), the penalties of disobedience as well as the rewards of obedience (ch. 28). So even at the point of the imminent fulfilment of the promise of land, the promise as a whole, in all its elements, has not become an inalienable possession of Israel's, but as much a challenge as a promise, a promise that can be threatened and even thwarted by its recipients. Only the fact that it is *Yahweh's* promise can create any confidence in its continuing fulfilment.

In sum, therefore, we have observed in this chapter that the divine promise to the patriarchs, while frequently alluded to in each of its forms throughout the Pentateuch, presents one or other of its elements more prominently in the successive books of the Pentateuch. As I noted in my statement of theme (Chapter 5), in Genesis it is the promise of progeny that has predominated, in Exodus and Leviticus the promise of the relationship of Yahweh and Israel, and in Numbers and Deuteronomy the promise of the land.

7

Prefatory Theme

Up to this point in the present study the chapters of the 'primaeval history' (Genesis 1–11) have been left almost entirely out of account. This has been partly for a logical reason: they concern a world in which the divine promise to the patriarchs has not yet been spoken, and so their theme—whatever it may be—can hardly be subsumed under that of the patriarchal promises and their (partial) fulfilments. The other reason is a logistic reason: there is so much to be said about the structure of these chapters, which themselves do not make their theme plain, that they need to be dealt with by themselves.

So the first task will be to consider what theme, if any, Genesis 1–11 in its present form has, and the second, to understand that theme in relationship to the theme of the rest of the Pentateuch.

a. The Theme of Genesis 1-11

Since the theme—if one exists—of these chapters can only be implicit, our method of search must be by trial and error, as I have suggested above in Chapter 2. Three themes, which have been proposed for these chapters, fall to be considered:

1. A Sin-Speech-Mitigation-Punishment Theme

The first theme to be investigated is realized in the plot or story pattern of the major narratives in Genesis 1–11. G. von Rad has pointed out how the narratives of the Fall, of Cain and Abel, of the 'sons of God', of the Flood and of the Tower of Babel each exhibit a movement from (a) human sin to (b) divine punishment to (c) divine forgiveness or mitigation of the punishment:

> God reacts to these outbreaks of human sin with severe judgements ... [Yet] the Yahwistic narrator shows something else along with the consequences of divine judgement ... Each time, in and after the judgement, God's preserving, forgiving will to save is revealed.[1]

Although von Rad does not state the theme in quite this fashion, he obviously understands the theme of these narratives to be the following. Whenever humans sin, God's response is just, and yet gracious; he punishes, yet he forgives. Since these are narratives about the human condition in general, and are not tied down to particular episodes in ancient historical actuality, the theme expresses a broad affirmation about the character of God's relationship with humankind.

Two questions immediately arise: (1) Can the narrative pattern exemplified in these narratives be differently, or better, analysed? (2) Are the *narratives* of Genesis 1–11 an adequate basis for establishing the theme of Genesis 1–11 as a whole?

To (1) we can reply, first, that Claus Westermann's analysis of the narrative pattern in these chapters[2] brings to light another significant element. He observes that there always intervenes between the act of sin and the act of punishment a divine *speech* announcing or deciding the penalty. Accordingly he draws up the following table analysing the elements of the major narratives:

	I. *Sin*	II. *Speech*	III. *Punishment*
1. Fall	3.6	3.14-19	3.22-24
2. Cain	4.8b	4.11-12	4.16b
3. Sons of God	6.1-2	6.3	—
4. Flood	6.5-7	6.5-7	7.6-24
5. Babel	11.4	11.6-7	11.8-9
6. (Canaan)	9.22	9.24-25	—

Westermann very properly sees theological significance in this recurrent element of the divine speech. It means, he says, first that God's acts of judgment are always related to a particular sin and so are the very opposite of arbitrary, secondly that there is but one God, who is responsible for woe and weal alike, and thirdly that it is the character of that God to be a judge and to hold himself responsible for detecting and punishing human sin.

But, secondly, we may reply to the prior question by observing that Westermann does not include within his analysis the important element of mitigation, to which von Rad has drawn attention. And neither Westermann nor von Rad has noted that this element of mitigation or grace occupies a significant place in the pattern of these narratives: it is always to be found *after* the speech of punishment and *before* the act of punishment. That is to say, God's grace or 'forgiving will to save' is not only revealed 'in and after the judgement', as von Rad says,[3] but even *before* the execution of judgment. So this fuller structure of the narratives may then be exposed thus:

	I. *Sin*	II. *Speech*	III. *Mitigation*	IV. *Punishment*
1. Fall	3.6	3.14-19	3.21	3.22-24
2. Cain	4.8	4.11-12	4.15	4.16
3. Sons of God	6.2	6.3	? 6.8, 18ff.	? 7.6-24
4. Flood	6.5, 11f.	6.7, 13-21	6.8, 18ff.	7.6-24
5. Babel	11.4	11.6f.	? 10.1-32	11.8

To observe that all the narratives of the primaeval history conform to a pattern does not destroy the individuality of the narratives, but rather highlights their distinctiveness. Some significant differences in fact exist among the various exemplifications of the overall pattern. In nos. 1 and 2 it is individuals who sin and are punished, in 3–5 it is communities. 1 and 2 contain the element of God's investigation of the crime, while in 3–5 the sins are public and in 3 and 5 God only needs to 'see' the crime (6.5, 12; 11.5). In 1 and 2 it is the same persons who sin, are punished, and are partly relieved of the severity of their punishment. In 3 a greater number than those who have sinned are punished, and it is uncertain whether there is any mitigation.[4] In

4 the vast majority of those who have sinned are punished and the mitigation takes effect only for one man and his family;[5] in 5 all those who have sinned are punished, and there is no direct mitigation.

These variations are not insignificant. Where God's relationship with individuals is concerned, his dealing can be highly personalized (note especially the differing punishments for the three principal actors in the Fall story). But where a whole community's relationship with God is involved, the operation of justice in punishment can sometimes be undifferentiated, as in the 'Sons of God' episode, where all humanity's life-span (or, it may be, the period before the Flood) is shortened because of the sins of the 'Sons of God', one presumes. But sometimes the effects of the punishment are differentiated, as in the Flood story, where Noah and his family escape. In each case, however, except perhaps for the last (the Tower of Babel), there is an outworking of the basic pattern of sin—speech—mitigation—punishment. Can this pattern, then, form the basis for a statement of the theme of Genesis 1–11?

That brings us to our question (2): Can the narratives alone form an adequate basis for establishing the theme of Genesis 1–11 as a whole? It is indeed correct that the theme of a narrative work often emerges from a consideration of its plot or narrative pattern, or, as could in principle be the case here, from a narrative pattern repeated in every episode of the narrative. But we still must ask whether the plot of the narratives of Genesis 1–11 can account for the presence within these chapters of the creation account (Gen. 1), the genealogies (4.17-26; 5; 11.10-26), and the table of nations (ch. 10)? I myself think it does not. If 'theme' is a statement of the content, structure and development of a work, as I have suggested above, the 'sin–speech–mitigation–punishment' pattern, significant though it is, can only be called a recurrent motif in the primaeval history, and not the unifying theme of Genesis 1–11 as a whole. G. von Rad himself, we should note, spoke only of the *Yahwistic* Primaeval History when developing his 'sin–punishment–mitigation' scheme; that is, he saw this theme as part of the work of the Yahwist author, not of the Priestly author who also contributed to Genesis 1–11. Although von Rad regarded the Yahwistic scheme as the foundation of the final canonical shape of Genesis 1–11, he never directly expressed his understanding of the significance of Genesis 1–11 in its final form, and so fell short of his own excellent goal of understanding the work 'as a whole with a consistent train of thought'.[6]

2. A Spread-of-Sin, Spread-of-Grace Theme

a. *Statement.* Another element of G. von Rad's understanding of the theme of Genesis 1–11 is the theme of the 'spread of sin', to which there corresponds increasingly severe punishment, along with a parallel spread of 'grace' on God's part.[7] That is to say: (1) From Eden to Babel by way of the sins of Cain, Lamech, the 'sons of God', and the generation of the Flood, there is an ever-growing 'avalanche' of sin, a 'continually widening chasm between man and God'. There is a movement from disobedience to murder, to reckless killing, to titanic lust, to total corruption and violence, to the full disruption of humanity. (2) God responds to the extension of human sin with increasingly severe punishment: from expulsion from the garden to expulsion from the tillable earth, to the limitation of human life, to the near annihilation of mankind, to the 'dissolution of mankind's unity'. (3) Nevertheless, these are also stories of divine grace: God not only punishes Adam and Eve, but also withholds the threatened penalty of death; he not only drives out Cain, but also puts his mark of protection upon him; not only sends the Flood, but saves the human race alive in preserving Noah and his family. Only in the case of the Babel narrative does it appear that the element of 'grace' is lacking—a subject to which we shall return later.

b. *Development.* Such a statement of the theme of Genesis 1–11 is initially open to the same objection as was raised above: it speaks only to the *narratives* of these chapters. However, in the case of this theme there is the possibility that it can be extended to include parts of Genesis 1–11 outside the main narratives, i.e. that it can account for the content, development and shape of the material as a whole. So let us consider the major elements of the primaeval history outside the main narratives. They are:

(1) *The creation account* (Gen. 1). The connection of this chapter with the spread of sin theme becomes clear if we accept the perspective of D. Kidner: he sees Genesis 1–11 as describing 'two opposite progressions: first, God's orderly creation, to its climax in man as a responsible and blessed being, and then the disintegrating work of sin, to its first great anticlimax in the corrupt world of the Flood, and its second in the folly of Babel'.[8] That is, the theme of the spread of sin is only the negative aspect of the overall theme, which remains yet to be defined. We may take this insight further and observe that the pattern according to which creation proceeds in ch. 1 is in fact the positive aspect of the sin–judgment motif: here it is a matter of obedience followed by blessing, not sin followed by curse. So, for example, light comes into being in prompt obedience to the word of God (1.3), whereupon the divine judgment is pronounced: God saw that it was good. The chapter as a whole moves toward 'blessing', first upon the living creatures (1.22), then upon the humans (1.28), and finally upon the seventh day (2.3). Genesis 1 is thus the positive counterpart to the remainder of the primaeval history (though the remainder is not unrelieved gloom).

(2) *The genealogies* (Gen. 4.17-26; 5; 11.10-26). Since the kind of theme appropriate to Genesis 1–11 is obviously theological, we may well wonder whether the genealogies can in any way be integrated with the overall theme of these chapters. The genealogies have indeed not usually been thought to serve some theological function, but have often been regarded simply as ancient material reproduced here only because of the chronological relationship of their contents to the narratives of Genesis 1–11.[9] Yet there are some clues in the narrative sections of Genesis 1–11 that point to the validity of a theological interpretation of the genealogies—that is, to the likelihood that the final author of the primaeval history intended them to express some theological

purpose.

The first clue lies in some statements about the multiplication of the human race. In 1.28 the procreation of humanity stands under divine command and blessing: 'And God blessed them, and God said unto them, "Be fruitful and multiply, and fill the earth" '. To the same effect are the statements by Eve at the birth of Cain and Seth: 'I have gained (*or,* created) a man with the help of Yahweh' (4.1),[10] and 'God has appointed for me another child' (4.25). Just as the birth of Eve's children is a token of the divine aid, so the whole growth of the human family witnessed by these genealogies is to be viewed under the sign of the divine blessing.[11]

The second clue to the theological significance of the genealogies is provided by their form. No reader of Genesis 5, to take one example, fails to be impressed by the recurrent phrase 'And he died', which baldly and emphatically concludes the entry for each of these antediluvians. The whole movement of the regular form of these notices is toward death. The form is:

1. When A lived x years, he begat B.
2. A lived after the birth of B *y* years, and had other sons and daughters.
3. All the days of A were *z* [*x* + *y*] years.
4. And he died.

Items 3 and 4, we can see, are logically unnecessary. They add nothing to the information given in items 1 and 2. Their function must be to emphasize a finality about each of these lives, as if to say: though possessed of an excess of vitality by ordinary human standards,[12] these men also die. Thus the thrust of the Genesis 5 genealogy is toward death, even though human life continues.

A further hint of progression toward death may be given by the diminishing life-spans attributed to the personages of the primaeval history. While the antediluvians usually live 800 or 900 years,[13] the generations after the Flood live ever shorter lives, from 600 years for Shem (11.10) to 205 for Terah (11.32).[14] This decline may perhaps be seen, as von Rad put it, as a deterioration of humanity's 'original wonderful vitality, a deterioration corresponding to his increasing distance from his starting point at creation'. Genesis 5, for example, could then be said to describe a 'transitional period, during which death caused by sin broke the powerful resistance of primitive human nature'.[15]

As for the genealogical material of ch. 4, its function within the primaeval history becomes clearly visible when it is viewed from the perspective of the spread of sin theme. The Cainite genealogy of 4.17-24 has the same dialectic significance as the Sethite genealogy of ch. 5.[16] In ch. 4, while the genealogy appears on the surface to be a list of the founders of the arts of civilization (the city, cattle-breeding, music, metal-working),[17] and was perhaps originally transmitted as such, it is made clear by the point to which the progress of civilization reaches, namely Lamech's tyrannous boast (4.23f.), that this has been a progress in sin as much as in civilization.[18] In the seven generations of the line of Cain history has seen a 'progress' from an impulsive act of murder to a deliberate reign of terror. But, by affixing the beginning of a Sethite genealogy (4.25f.) to the Cainite list, the author of Genesis 4 has affirmed that the world of humanity is not totally given over to the Cainite life-style. Even while the race of Cain is increasing in congenital violence, he means to say, elsewhere there is a line of humans who have begun to 'call on the name of Yahweh' (4.26).

Thus, whatever may have been the origin of the genealogies or their original function, the present form of Genesis 1–11 permits us to interpret them as displaying a theological purpose analogous to that outlined by von Rad for the narratives. Here also in the genealogies there is the monotonous reiteration of the fact of death, which increasingly encroaches upon life—a pessimistic note that corresponds to the narrative theme of the continuing spread of sin. But, as in the narratives, history is not simply a matter of sin and punishment; where sin abounds, grace much more abounds. Even though the divine grace is experienced not in dramatic acts of deliverance, as it is in the narratives, but in the steady silent expansion of human life, it is the divine grace all the same. To the grace that appoints for Eve another child to take the place of the dead Abel is owed also the furtherance of humankind's growth throughout the genealogy of Genesis 5; and to the grace that preserves the human race through the dramatic rescue of Noah and his family from the Flood is due also the repeopling of the earth after the Flood (Gen. 10).

(3) *The Table of Nations* (Gen. 10). It is a remarkable feature of the structure of the primaeval history that the Table of Nations (ch. 10) is located not after the story of the Tower of Babel (11.1-9) but before it. Since ch. 10 recounts the 'spreading' (*pārad*, vv. 5, 23) or 'scattering' (*pûṣ*, v. 18) of humans, 'each with their own language' (v. 5; cf. vv. 20, 31), it would seem more logically placed after 11.1-9, which recounts the 'scattering' (*pûṣ*) of humanity 'over the face of all the earth' and the division of languages.

A thematic explanation for this absence of chronological order is ready to hand in the 'spread-of-sin, spread-of-grace' theme. If the material of ch. 10 had followed the Babel story, the whole Table of Nations would have to be read under the sign of judgment; but where it stands it functions as the fulfilment of the divine command of 9.1, 'Be fruitful and multiply, and fill the earth', which looks back in its turn to 1.28. All this means that the final author of the primaeval history understands that the dispersal of the nations may be evaluated both positively (as in ch. 10) and negatively (as in ch. 11). Since Babel, humankind stands under both the blessing and the curse of God; the division of the peoples and their languages is both a token of the divine judgment and a natural concomitant of humanity's fulfilment of the divine command and so part of the divine 'blessing' (9.1). With this ambivalence in the relationship of God with humanity the primaeval history comes to a conclusion. The final author or redactor of the primaeval history has, by the sequence in which he has arranged his materials on the dispersal of humankind, made the same theological point as have the narratives and genealogies in the preceding chapters: that though the judgment of God rests upon humans as sinful, they experience not only his judgment but also his grace.

c. *Criticism.* So far the statement of the 'spread-of-sin' theme with which this section began has proved productive of insight into material that von Rad did not himself connect with the theme. But next we should consider whether there are any difficulties in regarding the 'spread-of-sin' theme as the unifying theme of these chapters.[19]

(1) While it may be readily granted that a 'spread' of sin and an intensification of punishment from Adam to Cain and from Cain to the generation of the Flood is clear, it may well be asked whether any such extension or intensification can be discerned when the Flood and the Babel narratives are compared. Can the theme of Genesis 1–11 properly be said to be the increasing spread of sin when the last exemplification of the theme, the Babel story, depicts neither a sin so drastic as that which brings on the Flood nor a punishment so severe and universal as the Flood?[20]

This issue will depend to some extent on how precisely the sins of Gen. 6.1-4 and 11.1-9 are understood. It is possible, for example, to interpret the sin of the 'sons of God' in 6.1-4 not, as is commonly thought, as the unnatural mixing of the divine and the human, but as a sin of violence on the purely human plane.[21] Then, if the sin of the 'sons of God', which is partly, though not wholly, the cause for the Flood, is perhaps not so fundamental as some interpreters have claimed, the sin of the tower-builders may not be so insignificant as at first sight appears. Their sin may be seen not as a mere expression of human self-importance and self-reliance, but as an act of *hybris,* matched in its defiance of God only by the first sin in the garden; like the eating of the forbidden fruit, the tower-building may be an assault on heaven, an attempt at self-divinization.[22] Such an interpretation is confirmed by the fact that, so understood, the primaeval history would exhibit the common literary technique of *inclusio,* with the final episode in the story of human sin repeating and balancing the first.

But if the sin of the generation of the Flood is not necessarily more heinous than that of the tower-builders, is the scattering of humankind a more severe punishment than the Flood? It may be replied that in two ways at least the scattering is more drastic than the Flood. First, the Flood left no permanent mark on humanity; though the generation of the Flood was destroyed, humankind was preserved, and continued to grow. The scattering of humankind, however, is of lasting effect. There are no survivors of Babel. Secondly, what is destroyed at Babel is the community of humankind as a family; hitherto, as the genealogies have witnessed, humanity is one family, and the Flood has only accentuated that fact by making one family in the narrowest sense of the word coterminous with humanity. But the punishment of Babel divides humans irrevocably from one another (as did also the first sin in its own way); now humankind is no longer one 'people' or 'kin-group' (*'am*, 11.6), but 'nations' (*gôyim*, 10.32).

In sum, this criticism of a theme of spread-of-sin from the Fall to Babel can be met by a more exact interpretation of the significance of the Flood and Babel narratives.

(2) Another criticism of the spread-of-sin theme from Eden to Babel arises from the opinion that it is Gen. 8.21 (at the close of the Yahwistic Flood narrative) and not the Babel story that brings the primaeval history to a close. In his influential study on this passage,[23] Rolf Rendtorff claims that this verse should be translated: 'I will no longer curse the earth', or 'I will no longer regard the earth as cursed, and treat it as such'. It is not, he maintains, that God will not *again* curse the earth, but that at 8.21 the period of the curse uttered by God in 3.17, 'Cursed is the ground because of you', is concluded. 'From now on it is no longer curse that rules the world, but blessing. The time of the curse is at an end, the time of blessing has arrived.'[24] Some who have followed Rendtorff's view have expressed the contrast rather less starkly. Thus W.M. Clark says, 'The power of that initial curse to work disruption is limited',[25] and T.E. Fretheim writes:

> The idea of blessing ... is here introduced for the first time (v. 22). Since the beginning of man's sin the curse has been

> predominant in the created order of things, leading to the catastrophe of the Flood. This will not continue to be the case. Now blessing stands alongside of the curse and begins to have its beneficial effects on the earth, breaking down the effects of the curse (3.17). This is made concretely evident for the first time in the following story (in J) of Noah and his vineyard.[26]

If this view is correct, there is of course no point in our search for a theme of Genesis 1–11, since those chapters do not form a literary unit.

The view of Rendtorff and his followers, however, does not appear to me to be well founded in its central contention.[27] The curse that will not again come upon the ground (8.21) is not the curse of 3.17. There the curse upon the ground was that it would bring forth thorns and thistles; and that curse is not said in 8.21 to be lifted, nor is it easy to see how the Yahwist, or any author, could have claimed from his own experience that it had in fact been lifted. In 8.21 the curse has been the smiting of the earth with a flood. It is true, as Rendtorff points out,[28] that the introduction to the Flood story does not specifically view the Flood as a 'curse', but that is not a very strong counter-argument to the plain structure of 8.21. Here the clause 'I will not again curse the earth' seems clearly parallel to 'I will not again smite all living beings',[29] as God has done by means of the Flood. There is indeed a verbal connection between 3.17 and 8.21 ('Cursed is the ground because of [*ba'ăbûr*] you' and 'I will not curse the ground because of [*ba'ăbûr*] humanity'), but the content of the two passages is different, and we are dealing simply with the repetition of a verbal motif which takes on new light in different settings.[30]

A further weakness in the view that 8.21 ends the period of the curse lies in its interpretation of the narrative of Noah's vineyard (9.20-27). According to W.M. Clark, that narrative 'does not convey the idea that wine relieves the toil of mankind, but rather is a verification that the curse has been lifted off the ground which can henceforth produce vineyards, a symbol of fertility.'[31] But this is to misunderstand the clear connection between the vineyard story and the birth-oracle of Noah in 5.29: 'Out of the ground, which Yahweh has cursed, this one [Noah] shall bring us relief from our work and from the toil of our hands'; that is, the 'relief out of the ground' is the discovery of the cultivation of the vine and the making of wine.[32] The curse is not lifted from the ground, but even the cursed ground can produce some comfort and enjoyment for humans. The pattern of punishment relieved by divine grace is visible here too, though it is not so explicitly spelled out as it is in some of the longer narratives.

It may finally be objected to the view of Rendtorff, especially as it is developed by Clark, that the remainder of the Yahwist's post-Flood primaeval history cannot be satisfactorily interpreted as belonging to an age of blessing rather than of curse. What immediately follows the story of Noah's drunkenness is not blessing but curse—the curse of Canaan (9.25ff.). And even though there is contained in this curse a blessing on Shem and Japheth, which is the first explicit blessing in the Yahwist's work, as Clark says (though not the first in the primaeval history as it now stands; cf. 1.22, 28; 2.8; 5.2; 9.1), the structure of vv. 25ff., which begin with 'Cursed be Canaan', and in which each blessing is followed with 'And let Canaan be his slave', shows that attention is focused on Canaan and the curse rather than on the blessing. Furthermore, it is difficult to see how Clark can interpret the vineyard and Babel narratives as a 'recapitulation of the events prior to the flood . . . a story of sin on the individual level followed by a story in which sin threatens to reach cosmic dimensions again' without understanding them as developing a 'spread-of-sin' theme, which is hardly appropriate for the age of blessing.[33]

It seems incorrect, therefore, to regard Gen. 8.22 as marking the major turning-point in the Yahwist's primaeval history; the 'spread-of-sin' theme both includes the Flood and extends beyond it.

(3) A quite different suggestion, which would cast doubt on the 'spread-of-sin' as the unifying theme of Genesis 1–11, is that of W. Brueggemann in his study, 'David and his Theologian'.[34] He argues that the sequence of episodes in the Yahwistic material

of Genesis 1–11 is 'dependent upon the career of the sons of David in the quest for the throne'.[35] The four stories of sin in Genesis 3–11 (Adam and Eve; Cain and Abel; Noah and the Flood; the Tower of Babel) correspond, he argues, to the four major episodes of the 'Succession Narrative' of 2 Samuel 9–20 and 1 Kings 1–2 (David and Bathsheba; Amnon and Absalom; Absalom and David; Solomon and David). *Prima facie,* if this is so, the structure of Genesis 1–11 is essentially (at least as far as the Yahwistic material is concerned) shaped by the course of Israelite history in the tenth century BCE and not by a conceptual theme such as the 'spread-of-sin'.

Brueggemann is indeed able to point to many striking correspondences of language and motif between the primaeval history and the Succession Narrative. But two considerations make his general thesis rather unlikely, in my opinion:[36] (i) The correspondence between Absalom's rebellion and the Flood story is not very strong,[37] as Brueggemann himself candidly acknowledges;[38] and one major disruption of the pattern spoils the argument about sequence, which is crucial to the present discussion. Even if some narratives in Genesis 1–11 are reflections of the Davidic history, the sequence of those narratives is not clearly dependent upon it. (ii) Striking parallels of motif and language can also be traced between the Succession Narrative and other sections of the Yahwistic work,[39] and so a special relationship with Genesis 1–11 cannot be claimed.[40]

Furthermore, even if there is a sequential correspondence between the two works, there is no clear evidence that the Davidic narrative is prior to the primaeval history, nor that the telling of the David story itself has not been influenced—in its selection of episodes and in its language—by the primaeval history.[41] It is unnecessary, therefore, to regard Brueggemann's view, stimulating though it is, as an obstacle to uncovering a conceptual link between the narratives of Genesis 1–11, namely the 'spread-of-sin' theme.

To summarize to this point: The theme of the 'spread-of-sin' accounts for the vast majority of the content of Genesis 1–11.

It is visible, not only in the narratives, but also in other literary types in these chapters. It is more than probable that, even if this suggested theme alone does not adequately express the thrust of Genesis 1–11, its pervasiveness ensures that it will have to be taken into account in any statement of theme in the primaeval history.

3. A Creation-Uncreation-Re-creation Theme

We have already noted that the position of the Flood episode within Genesis 1–11 has given rise to some criticisms of the 'spread-of sin' theme. While those criticisms can be met, the fact remains that the Flood narrative does not function simply as yet a further stage in the development of human sin, but imports concepts of 'end' and 're-creation' into the primaeval history.[42] When Genesis 1 is also taken into consideration, some case can be made out for suggesting that the theme of the primaeval history is 'creation—uncreation—re-creation'.

It is very plain that the Flood is represented not just as a punishment for the sin of the generation of the Flood, but as a reversal of creation—'uncreation', as Joseph Blenkinsopp has put it. 'The world in which order first arose out of a primaeval watery chaos is now reduced to the watery chaos out of which it arose—chaos-come-again.'[43] While Genesis 1 depicts creation as largely a matter of separation and distinction, Genesis 6f. portrays the annihilation of distinctions. If in Gen. 1.6ff. a firmament is established to keep the heavenly waters from falling upon the earth except in properly regulated measure, 7.11 has the 'windows of heaven' opening to obliterate this primal distinction. Similarly, the distinction between the lower waters and the earth in 1.9 is done away with by the breaking forth through the earth of the 'fountains of the great deep' (7.11). The binary nature of created existence gives way to the formlessness of the 'waste and void' (*tōhû wābōhû*) that existed before creation. And significantly, the destruction follows much the same sequence as the creation: earth, birds, cattle, wild animals, swarming creatures, humans (7.21).

Re-creation occurs, in the first place, by the renewed separation of sea and land: the waters recede from and dry up from the earth (8.3, 7, 13). Then comes the renewal of the divine order to living beings to 'breed, be fruitful, and multiply' (8.17). There follows God's guarantee of the binary structure of existence: seedtime and harvest, cold and heat, summer and winter, day and night are re-established (8.22). Finally, the creation ordinances are re-announced, albeit in somewhat altered form (9.1-7),[44] the separation of sea and land—a fundamental element in the creative process (1.9ff.)—is assured (9.8-17), and humankind begins to be re-created (by procreation, ch. 10) and to fill the earth at God's command (10.32).[45]

As for the intervening material of Genesis 1–11 between creation and flood, when it is viewed from the perspective of the theme 'creation—uncreation—re-creation' new understandings emerge. Chief among them is the recognition that chs. 3–6 are not simply the story of human sin matched by divine grace, but the story of the undoing of creation. The flood is only the final stage in a process of cosmic disintegration that began in Eden. While ch. 1 views reality as an ordered pattern that is confused by the flood, chs. 2–3 see reality as a network of elemental unions that become disintegrated throughout the course of the narrative from Eden to the Flood.

Thus, in Genesis 2, as in Genesis 1, reality has a binary structure. Here, however, creation has not proceeded by distinction and separation, but by the forging of bonds: between humans and the soil, humans and the animals, the man and the woman, humanity and God. In ch. 3 the relationship of harmony between each of these pairs is disrupted. The communion between God and the man who breathes God's breath (2.7) has become the legal relationship of accuser and defendant (3.9ff.); the relationship of man and woman as 'one flesh' (2.24) has soured into mutual recrimination (3.12); the bond of humanity (*'ādām*) with the soil (*'ădāmâ*) from which he was built has been supplanted by 'an alienation that expresses itself in a silent, dogged struggle between man and sod'[46] (3.17ff.); the harmonious relationship of humans with beast in which the human is the acknowledged master (2.19ff.) has become a perpetual struggle of intransigent foes (3.15). In Genesis 4 another union, of twin (?)[47] brothers, which might have been expected to be paradigmatic of human friendship,[48] is broken by the ultimate act of enmity, murder. Cain is further alienated from the soil, by being driven out from the tillable earth (4.11), and the bond between humans and the soil is further loosened. The disintegration of the most intimate bond of all—of humans with their own breath (which is also the divine breath, 2.7)—first sets in with the murders by Cain and Lamech (4.8, 23), broadens its scope with the successive deaths of each descendant of Adam in the genealogy of ch. 5, and reaches its climax with the simultaneous death of almost the whole of humankind in ch. 7. The destruction of humanity is significantly expressed in language reminiscent of creation: Yahweh determines that he will 'blot out humanity whom I have created' (6.7), whereupon 'all in whose nostrils was the breath of the spirit of life (*nišmat-rûaḥ ḥayyîm*)' died (7.22), an echo of Yahweh Elohim's breathing into the man's nostrils the 'breath of life (*nišmat ḥayyîm*)' (2.7). With this, the creation of humanity is undone.

A new movement toward uncreation viewed as the dissolution of unities begins again directly after the Flood. Ham's incest with his mother—if that is the significance of 9.20-27[49]—strikes at the bond between man and woman (2.23f.), and the scattering of humankind after the building of Babel (11.9) is a potent symbol of the disintegration of humankind's unity. The tendency of humans has not been changed by the Flood: the 'imagination of the human heart is evil from its youth' (8.21) as much after the Flood as before it.

So there can be little doubt that the theme 'creation—uncreation—re-creation' is firmly fixed in Genesis 1–11, and needs to be taken into account in our general statement of the theme of these chapters as the preface to the Pentateuch.

4. Conclusion

Having considered three suggested themes for Genesis 1–11 (the sin—speech—mitigation—punishment pattern; the spread-of-sin, spread-of-grace theme; the creation—uncreation—re-creation theme), I conclude that the first is too unrepresentative of the total content of the primaeval history to be regarded as part of its theme (though it is, obviously, a recurrent motif), while the second and third satisfactorily fulfil the condition for 'theme' of accounting for the content, shape and development of the material. I would therefore suggest that any adequate total statement of the theme of these chapters should allow for both proposed themes. However, if they are combined, two quite different possible readings of Genesis 1–11 emerge. The theme of the primaeval history could be said to be either:

(a) Humankind tends to destroy what God has made good. Even when God forgives human sin and mitigates the punishment, sin continues to spread, to the point where the world suffers uncreation. And even when God makes a fresh start, turning his back on uncreation forever, the human tendency to sin immediately becomes manifest. Or:

(b) No matter how drastic human sin becomes, destroying what God has made good and bringing the world to the brink of uncreation, God's grace never fails to deliver humankind from the consequences of their sin. Even when humanity responds to a fresh start with the old pattern of sin, God's commitment to his world stands firm, and sinful humans experience the favour of God as well as his righteous judgment.[50]

It does not appear obvious from Genesis 1–11 itself that one or other of these readings is inappropriate. The primaeval history viewed in isolation from the rest of the Pentateuch is therefore utterly ambiguous in its central statement. But by considering it in relationship with the remainder of the Pentateuch it becomes possible, I believe, both to opt decisively for one of the above formulations of theme, and at the same time to add a new dimension to the overall theme of the Pentateuch itself as it has been stated in Chapter 4 above and explored in Chapter 6 above.

b. The Theme of Genesis 1–11 in Relationship to the Theme of the Pentateuch

At this point it becomes necessary to bring into the discussion an issue that I have previously left on one side, namely the precise terminus of the primaeval history. Hitherto I have been able to speak rather loosely of 'Genesis 1–11', but now the precise conclusion of this literary unit becomes critical. If it concludes with the last narrative of these chapters (11.1-9), some colour is lent to von Rad's claim (rather strongly expressed) that the absence of the mitigation element in the Babel story means that 'the whole primeval history ... seems to break off in strict dissonance' and that the question arises: 'Is God's gracious forbearance now exhausted; has God rejected the nations in wrath forever?'[51] A sharp disjunction can then be made between universal history (Gen. 1–11) and 'salvation history' (Gen. 12 onward), with the themes of the two units being set in contrast: universal history leads only to judgment, whereas the narrowing of vision to Abraham opens the way for an era of blessing, that is, for salvation history. Statement (a) of the theme of the primaeval history would thus appear to be appropriate.

However, it is most significant that there is no clear-cut break at the end of the Babel story. It is true that the Abraham material begins a new section of the Pentateuch, but the precise beginning of the Abraham material—and therewith the conclusion of the pre-Abrahamic material—cannot be determined.[52] In the final form of Genesis, therefore, there is at no point a break between primaeval and patriarchal history. What follows immediately upon the Babel story (11.1-9) is the genealogical table leading from Shem to Terah (11.10-26). But who Shem is can be learned only from the Table of Nations, where his family is detailed 'according to their families, languages, lands and nations' (10.21-31), or from the Noah story, where Shem is the son upon whom Noah has pronounced the blessing: 'Blessed by Yahweh my God be Shem' (9.26). So the Shem genealogy is firmly linked into the primaeval history. On the other hand, it is plain that the goal of the genealogy is Abram (11.26-30). Its function is equally to trace the ancestry of Abram—so it is attached to what follows—*and* to follow the line of descent from Shem—so it is attached to what precedes.

Now, since we find between the pre-patriarchal (primaeval) history and the patriarchal history a developed transitional passage, it is improbable that the two units are meant to be seen as opposed to one another thematically. Had they been sharply juxtaposed, it might have been a different matter (I have argued above that Genesis 1 is to be contrasted with chs. 2–11 in this way[53]). But as it is, since the patriarchal history—and the other books of the Pentateuch—unfold the fulfilment of the divine promise (Gen. 12.23; etc.), it is most likely that a positive reading of Genesis 1–11, as sketched in statement (b) above, is appropriate. Read by itself, the primaeval history defined as Gen. 1.1—11.5 could well have a negative tendency (statement [a] above); but once it is followed by the patriarchal and Pentateuchal history and linked by a developed transitional passage, such a tendency is totally reversed.

The patriarchal (or, Pentateuchal) narratives can then function as the 'mitigation' element of the Babel story, and what is more, the divine promise to the patriarchs then demands to be read in conjunction with Genesis 1—as a re-affirmation of the divine intentions for humanity.[54] Alongside the patriarchal promise of descendants, land, and divine-human relationship, the whole promise being categorized as 'blessing', we may align Genesis 1.26ff. Here the primal divine utterance consists of these commands and statements: (a) 'be fruitful and multiply'; (b) 'fill the earth (? land) and master it'; (c) 'God created humanity in his own image'; (d) 'God blessed them'. To be sure, the divine word now comes to Abram, and not to humankind, but Genesis 12.3, however interpreted, envisages some kind of overspill of blessing beyond the Abrahamic family.[55] More important than the *limitations* of the primal divine command/promise is its *re-affirmation* or re-application. Just as with the Flood story, it no longer matters that humankind once came close to extermination, and what really matters is the re-affirmation of the divine speech of ch. 1 in ch. 9, so also here, no fundamental shift in God's relation to humanity has occurred—though it must be conceded that its outworking, in being confined primarily to the Abrahamic family, proceeds in a significantly different way from that envisaged in ch. 1.

To link the primaeval history with the patriarchal narrative specifies the thrust of the primaeval history; it cannot be viewed negatively since it is the prelude to the promises and their fulfilment. But the dark side of the primaeval history still remains. In itself it may be read as a story of how things go wrong when humans take the initiatives; humankind tends to destroy what God has made good. Perhaps only the addition of a divine promise (Gen. 12) to a divine command (ch. 1) can counteract that tendency.

8

Divergences

In order to highlight the statement of theme in the Pentateuch in this book, I want in this chapter to consider some statements of theme that have been made by two other scholars (G. von Rad, B.T. Dahlberg), and to examine one book of the Pentateuch in which hitherto no unifying theme has been discerned.

a. G. von Rad

Since some elements in my analysis of the theme of the Pentateuch bear a resemblance to the work of G. von Rad—the only scholar I know who has seriously concerned himself with the structure of the Pentateuch in its final form—it is useful and necessary for me to make clear the divergence between von Rad's understanding and my own.

Von Rad's study of this topic in his *Old Testament Theology*[1] is presented, not unexpectedly, in a genetic form; that is, he deals first with the structure of the sources of the Pentateuch (or rather, for him, the Hexateuch) and only secondarily with the final form of the text. His exposition develops in three stages:

1. The structure of the JE work (that is, the literary work that combined the documents of the Yahwist and the Elohist) is laid down by the two covenants mentioned in JE, the patriarchal and the Sinaitic covenants. While the traditions of the two were originally separate, and while E nuances the patriarchal covenant differently from J in laying greater emphasis upon human responsibility and decision, the covenants play a particularly significant role in the structure of the JE work. But it is principally one element—the promise of land—in one of the

covenants, the patriarchal, that performs a structural function. For von Rad, this promise is the 'most prominent item in the covenant with the patriarchs'[2] and 'the most conspicuous binding factor in the work JE',[3] a 'colossal arch spanning the time from the promise of a land in the ancient promise to the ancestors to the fulfilment of the same promise in the days of Joshua'.[4]

2. Secondly, von Rad observes that P (the Priestly work) is constructed somewhat differently, and so contributes new emphases to the Hexateuch. P knows of two covenants also, but they are those with Noah and Abraham (not the patriarchal and Sinaitic covenants). The content of the covenant with Abraham is a threefold promise: (1) Abraham is to become a people; (2) there will exist a new relationship to God; (3) Abraham and his seed will take possession of a land.[5]

3. Thirdly, when JE and P were combined in the final form of the Hexateuch, a structural division into periods emerged: (1) from creation to the flood; (2) from the covenant with Noah to the call of Abraham; (3) from the covenant with Abraham to the occupation of Canaan. Within this third period (though von Rad does not make this entirely clear) stands the three-fold promise with its fulfilments, 'the entire mass of the Hexateuch traditions [being] set beneath a threefold arch of promise and fulfilment':[6] the promise of progeny is fulfilled in Egypt, the promise of a divine relationship at Sinai, the promise of land under Joshua.

Instructive though this analysis is, I find that my own approach diverges from it in several crucial respects:

1. It seems that to comprehend the material of the Pentateuch (or Hexateuch) as a whole it is methodologically sounder to begin from the final form of the text rather than from its antecedents, especially when those antecedent sources are, more or less, hypothetical.

2. It is far from clear that the final form of the Pentateuch is structured by periods, each introduced by a covenant (it is uncertain whether or not von Rad envisaged the first period as initiated by a covenant with Adam).[7] For von Rad, to 'organize' the Hexateuchal history is unquestioningly assumed to be a

matter of 'divid[ing] it into periods'.[8] That need not be so at all, and I, for my part, have tried to show that the material is organized according to thematic elements in the promise.

3. I do not see any reason to emphasize the land as 'the most prominent item in the covenant with the patriarchs'.[9] Von Rad is led to regard it as such since the promise and fulfilment of the land effectively begin and end the Hexateuch, and so for him it is 'the most conspicuous binding factor not only in the work JE, but also in the Hexateuch in its final form'.[10] But is that enough to make it '*the* most prominent item in the covenant'? And what if there is no such thing as a Hexateuch?

4. The very existence of a Hexateuch seems to me highly debatable. It is one thing to decide that sources for the Pentateuch like J or P concluded with an account of the conquest, or that credal statements like Deut. 26.5-9, which could conceivably have formed the nucleus of the present canonical history, contained a reference to the conquest, but quite another thing to maintain that there ever was a Hexateuch that consisted of the Pentateuch plus Joshua in more or less the final form of those books. It is very hard to reconcile the work of the Deuteronomist, who in Joshua 'welded together ... highly dissimilar elements'[11] to form our present book, with the work of the Priestly redactor responsible for the remainder of the Hexateuch.

5. Unlike the Hexateuch, which can claim no higher status than that of a scholarly hypothesis, the Pentateuch is, and already was in post-exilic times at the latest, a concrete reality that did *not* conclude its narrative with the conquest. The limits of the Pentateuch as contrasted with a Hexateuch make a vast difference to the question of theme. Thus, for example, for von Rad, the *Hexateuch* told a story of a divine promise that was visibly fulfilled in history (cf. Josh. 21.43ff.); 'in consequence', von Rad writes, 'any new impulse in the saving history could only begin from Jahweh's addressing Israel anew—but at this stage such an impulse lies beyond the horizon'.[12] With the *Pentateuch,* however, the way is open and the expectation is entertained of a forthcoming fulfilment of a promise made long ago and hitherto

fulfilled only embryonically and inadequately.

6. Von Rad's analysis of the structure of the Pentateuch, whether by the system of periods or by the schema of a three-fold promise and its fulfilments, relates only to certain principal events in the corpus of the Hexateuch. The exposition presented above, on the other hand, attempts to account thematically for the content and structure of the various books of the Pentateuch in detail, and thereby to offer, in a proper literary sense, a statement of the theme of the work as a whole.

b. B.T. Dahlberg

In a brief article Bruce T. Dahlberg has been motivated by many of the same concerns that have stimulated my own study, and has given us a perceptive paper 'On Recognizing the Unity of Genesis'.[13] Like my own view, Dahlberg's holistic perspective, which he calls 'macroanalysis', does not arise from hostility to source analysis of the Pentateuch, but attempts to give an account of the work in its final shape. His conclusion is that Genesis, 'taken as a whole and by itself, offers itself as a unified work of literary art; that is to say, it is a unitary composition thematically developed and integrated from beginning to end'.[14]

Dahlberg's primary insight is that the Joseph narrative in chs. 37–50 acts as a balance and foil to the primaeval history of chs. 1–11. 'Joseph appears to have been drawn intentionally as a antitype to Adam and ... to other main representatives of humanity who figure in chapters 1 through 11.'[15] Thus Joseph's response to his brothers, 'Fear not, for am I in the place of God? As for you, you meant evil against me, but God meant it for good, to bring it about as at this day that a great people should be kept alive' (50.19-20), recalls the phrases from the primaeval history, 'you will be like God', 'knowing good and evil', 'you will not die' (3.5). Joseph's expulsion from Canaan parallels the expulsion from Eden, but the movement away from life is reversed in his being sent by God into Egypt 'to preserve life' (45.5-8). The universal famine of the Joseph story is a counterpart to the primaeval universal deluge; the strife between Joseph and his brothers, which is resolved in reconciliation, brings to a happy conclusion the fraternal rivalry that begins with Cain and Abel and runs throughout the patriarchal stories. And in Joseph there is in fact explicitly fulfilled for the first time the promise to the patriarchs of their being a blessing to the peoples of the earth (12.3; 28.15): 'Yahweh blessed the Egyptian's house for Joseph's sake' (39.5).[16] The Joseph narrative does not function, therefore, primarily as a *bridge* between the patriarchal narratives and the exodus material, as is commonly thought,,[17] but as an *inclusio* for the book of Genesis. Genesis thus 'celebrates a divine deliverance that takes place in Egypt and *before* the Exodus' and is 'a narrative that is meaningful and complete in itself'.[18]

Naturally, some of the links Dahlberg sees between the Joseph narrative and other parts of Genesis are more convincing than others, but assuming for the sake of argument that he has made out his case, I must ask: What implications does it have for my own view of the overall theme of the Pentateuch?

Dahlberg's most constructive insight, in so far as the analogies between the primaeval history and the Joseph story are not illusory or accidental, is that the Joseph story functions as a redemption or reversal of the disastrous tendency of the primaeval history. Yet the Joseph narrative, which leaves the descendants of Abraham exiles in Egypt, can only be a merely provisional and low key riposte to Genesis 1–11; for Joseph's bones have yet to be carried up out of Egypt into the land sworn to the forefathers (50.25). Nothing is *solved* by the Joseph story; but it brings to expression motifs out of the primaeval history that will be more fully developed in the Pentateuchal narrative as a whole. What is absent from Dahlberg's presentation is a sufficiently deep recognition of the movement set in train by the divine promise. He justifiably compares Genesis to the orchestral overture to a dramatic opera, the overture being not only the introduction but also a survey in prospect of all the major themes.[19] But if our concern reaches, as it does in the present study, beyond the overture, Genesis must also be regarded as the mainspring of the action, and as the development of the first element of the divine promise, while the Joseph story must be recognized not only as a foil to Genesis 1–11 but also as a bridge to the remainder of the Pentateuch.

c. Numbers

Purely by way of example to illustrate the difference a recognition of theme as has been expounded in this book makes to one's reading of the Pentateuch, we may observe the attitudes of commentators to one Pentateuchal book, Numbers.

All would agree with the remark of B.A. Levine that 'Numbers is the least coherent of all the Torah books',[20] and it must be admitted that there are several chapters whose presence in the book cannot easily be related to the theme of the land—which I have proposed as the dominant theme both of Numbers and of Deuteronomy. Yet more in the book is connected with that theme than is recognized, for example, in the commentary of N.H. Snaith. His analysis of the book is simply:

1. 1.1–10.10 What Happened at Sinai
2. 10.11–20.13 What Happened in the Wilderness
3. 20.14–36.13 What Happened from Kadesh to the Plains of Moab.[21]

That bare geographical analysis of the contents, correct enough though it is, tells us nothing of the direction of the book or of what I believe to be its central concern.

G.B. Gray accorded the book even less coherence. It 'possesses no unity of subject', he said; it is 'a section somewhat mechanically cut out of the whole of which it forms a part'; its first element (1.1–10.10) 'may be regarded as an appendix to the Books of Exodus and Leviticus'. In fact, he says, 'Exodus, Leviticus, and Numbers might have been much more suitably, though very unequally, divided as follows: (1) Ex. 1–18: The Exodus from Egypt to Sinai; (2) Ex. 19—Nu. 10.10: Sinai; (3) Nu. 10.11–36.13: From Sinai to the Jordan'.[22] Here the assumption is more explicit that the theme of Exodus to Numbers is nothing more than the sequence of events arranged by place; so the commentator is unable to see any reason for the fact that the book begins in the middle of the Sinai account. Gray did allow, it must be said, that the material of 10.11–36.13 does evidence a 'unity of subject'; but he meant by that only 'the fortunes of the Israelites after leaving Sinai ... up to the point at which they are ready to enter and conquer the Land of Promise'.[23] Again, we have a statement of plot rather than of theme.

To take yet another commentator, H. Holzinger concluded that 'The book as a whole is decidedly not a delightful literary achievement. It lacks flow and coherence.'[24] A.R.S. Kennedy similarly wrote that 'the present arrangement of the whole is, to the western mind at least, confused and illogical'.[25] I for my part certainly do not pretend to understand in detail the disposition of material in the book, but if we recognize that the beginning of Numbers signals a shift of focus to a new element in the Pentateuchal theme it changes our attitude to the book entirely. Not only is the structure of the book itself illuminated, but also it becomes clear that it is by no means the conglomeration of unrelated matters that former commentators have thought it to be.[26] Rather, Numbers establishes from its very beginning the thematic element of the land as the end to which everything drives, and its matter and movement are consistently oriented toward that goal.

9

Literary History

Now that we have taken a synoptic view of the theme of the Pentateuch as a whole, we are in a position to make historical enquiries about how that particular theme came to be the theme of the Pentateuch. It is hardly necessary to say that this method of procedure conflicts with that of virtually all other Pentateuchal scholars, or that I think my method, of working from the known to the (relatively) unknown, is superior. This is not the place for an argument about the merits of rival methodologies; it will be enough if the application of my method yields interesting and fruitful results.

It will be adequate for our purposes if in tracing the literary history of the theme of the Pentateuch we adopt the still prevailing four-document hypothesis of Pentateuchal origins. Certainly if the 'new Pentateuchal criticism', as represented by R. Rendtorff, H.H. Schmid, and J. van Seters among others,[1] gains ground, it would be necessary to formulate a new statement of the history of the theme. My main concern here is not to attempt a definitive statement of the pre-history of the Pentateuchal theme, but to show that my method does not preclude interest in the history of traditions and that in fact the significant moments in what may be postulated as the historical development of the Pentateuchal material stand out the more clearly if the final shape of the work is analysed first—not last.

Two aspects at least of the final theme of the Pentateuch deserve to have their ancestry traced: (a) the concept of a promise, which imports an element of expectation into the Pentateuchal material; (b) the concept of the non-fulfilment, or more exactly, an only partial fulfilment, of the patriarchal promises.

9. Literary History

a. The Concept of a Promise

The promise of Gen. 12.1-3 is almost universally ascribed to the Yahwist, and in addition the consensus of opinion is that the Yahwist's work concluded with, or at any rate contained, the fulfilment of the promise of land. G. Fohrer, for example, finds it 'incomprehensible that the source strata should not have contained a final account of the occupation',[2] while O. Kaiser remarks that 'there can be no argument whether the Yahwist narrated a conquest of the land to the west of the Jordan, but only whether his account is preserved' (that is to say, in Joshua).[3]

But although the promises and their fulfilment are assigned to the Yahwist, it is comparatively rare to find scholars locating the theme of the Yahwist's work in the promises and their fulfilment. O. Eissfeldt is content to detect in J (the Yahwist) 'a spirit of enthusiastic cultus and acceptance of agricultural life, and of national-political power and cultus', 'a proud and grateful delight in people, land, cultus and kingdom, exalted and unshattered'.[4] A. Weiser, it is true, goes somewhat deeper, detecting in the work a 'fundamental note' which is 'the accomplishment of the divine plan of salvation in defiance of all human obstacles, fears and hopes'; the 'basic conception' is that 'the people are preserved in face of the might of their enemies and in spite of the repeated rebellion of Israel ... The story serves to demonstrate the ascendancy of God in his power'.[5] But Weiser does not relate the divine plan that becomes fulfilled to the promise to the patriarchs.

For some other scholars, however, the promise and its fulfilment is thematically significant. For Noth, the promise of the land formed part of the 'groundwork' of the patriarchal tradition from the beginning, and in combination with the other 'themes' of the Pentateuch, especially that of 'guidance into the arable land', brought into being the 'great historical thread of 'promise and fulfilment' which binds together the entire work from beginning to end.[6] For von Rad also the promise is seen as 'the most conspicuous binding factor ... in the work JE',[7] though he also regards the two covenants, the Abrahamic and the Sinaitic, as 'what lay down the lines of the whole work of JE',[8] and it is not clear what the connection between the 'binding factor' and 'what lays down the lines' is. Again, as in Noth's work, the promise is understood predominantly as the promise of land, so that in these studies we are put on the track of recognizing at least in the land-promise and its fulfilment the theme of the Yahwist (whom we need not separate too distinctly from JE, in von Rad's opinion).

A much more specific understanding of the patriarchal promise, especially in its formulation in Gen. 12.1-3, as the theme of the Yahwist's work, comes to expression in the work of H.W. Wolff.[9] Wolff finds the promise of blessing, rather than the promise of land or progeny, to be the kernel of Gen. 12.1-3, and he nuances the matter of its fulfilment in a way that we must take up a little later on. Others, however, like J. Hoftijzer,[10] have regarded the promise motifs in the patriarchal narratives as largely secondary, and the current trend seems to be to investigate the origins of the individual elements separately, without relating the results of such investigation too closely to the conventional documentary sources (so, for example, C. Westermann[11]).

Much closer to my own concern here, and much more relevant to our quest for the origin of the theme of the Pentateuch is, an incidental remark of R.E. Clements: in Gen. 12.1-3, he writes, we have a three-fold promise which becomes a dominant motif of the Yahwist's work, and 'The whole of the Yahwist's epic is constructed around this *tria* of promises'.[12] That, however, seems to be as far as anyone in the current scholarly literature goes towards locating the *theme* of the Yahwist's work in the pattern of the promises and their fulfilments. It is worth considering, by those who have not stamped the Yahwist out of existence, whether the initial insight of Noth and von Rad may not deserve expansion, so that the theme of the Yahwist's work (from Genesis 12 onward, at any rate) may be viewed as the elaboration and fulfilment of the *three-fold* promise to the patriarchs.

If we move on now to the next in sequence of the Pentateuchal sources, according to the conventional hypothesis (I leave aside the source E), we find in D (more or less equivalent to Deuteronomy)[13] that—although the concept of promise and fulfilment could hardly be claimed to be its theme—the promise made to the ancestors is very much in the foreground (e.g. 1.8; 6.3, 10, 18, 23). Yet the demand for Israel's *obedience* is equally evident. So the note of expectation in Deuteronomy is not an entirely reassuring one, for Israel has before it not only the possibility of blessing, but also of curse (ch. 28); set before it is life and good, but also death and evil (30.15, 19f.). In Deuteronomy, which, as von Rad remarked, 'has grown with the generations', accompanying Israel as 'a constantly present word of God',[14] Israel 'lives in a present of decision'.[15] The promise that Israel will take the land is not in much doubt, but the promise that Yahweh will continue to be their God seems dangerously open to disappointment, and the promise of a continuing posterity could equally well come to an untimely end (30.17f.).

To turn now to the Priestly Work, we observe that it, like the Pentateuch itself, has not often been viewed as a comprehensive whole with a single determinative theme; the variety of its materials has foreclosed that possibility for most scholars. Thus while the *contents* of P can be listed, and its characteristic theology can be depicted, most scholars would not go further than declaring it to be 'a planned account extending from the creation of the world to the death of Moses'[16] (if such is indeed its conclusion). Two recent studies, however, have attempted to discern a theme that binds the whole work together.

According to W. Brueggemann, the central 'kerygmatic assertion' of P is the blessing declaration of Gen. 1.28: 'And God blessed them and God said to them: Be fruitful and multiply; and fill the earth and subdue it and have dominion'.[17] The five imperative verbs are 'not so much commands as authorizations by which the people are empowered to believe and act toward the future'.[18] They state the intention of God for the well-being and prosperity of those to whom they are addressed: humankind in the first place, but Israel of the exile in the historical circumstance of their composition. Brueggemann goes on to argue for the origin of this central affirmation of P in the conquest traditions of Deuteronomy, but whether or not that is so, what is significant is that Brueggemann understands the Priestly Work to be structured upon a command that looks toward a distant future. For P it is not the *promise* to the patriarchs but a divine *command* at creation that points toward land, posterity and blessing. The promise has been transposed into a different key.

In a later study,[19] Joseph Blenkinsopp moves from an examination of the conclusion-formulae in P to the view that P is structured by three decisive moments in its history: (i) the creation of the world; (ii) the construction of the sanctuary; (iii) the establishment of the sanctuary in the land and the division of the land among the tribes. In each case a solemn conclusion formula is used (Gen. 2.1f.; Exod. 39.32; 40.33; Josh. 19.51), a heightened form of the execution-formulae common in P (e.g. 'X did according to all that Yahweh [God] commanded him'). In every case the conclusion or execution formula indicates the completion of a command from God. Though in almost every important respect, including the question of the end of the P document, Blenkinsopp differs from Brueggemann, we may note with interest that Blenkinsopp's perception of P as structured on a pattern of command and fulfilment is not entirely dissimilar to the old Yahwist pattern of promise leading to fulfilment; for though P uses the terminology of 'command' rather than 'promise' it certainly does not imply that the command can be fulfilled by human effort alone without the divine initiative.[20]

So the element of promise, the first element in our statement of the theme of the Pentateuch whose literary history we are investigating, is to be found, in one form or another, in the three major sources of the Pentateuch.[21] This is not the case primarily because of literary influence, I would suggest, nor even because J/JE determined the fundamental shape of the Pentateuch, but because of remembered Israelite experience of its canonical history as movement toward a goal that had been established by a divine initiative.

b. The Concept of the Partial Fulfilment of the Promise

The second important element in our statement of the Pentateuch's theme, namely the non-fulfilment, or at least the merely partial fulfilment, of the initiating divine promise, also has an interesting history.

To begin again with the Yahwist, we observe that the majority opinion, despite some notable dissentients, is that the Yahwist's work originally concluded with a story of the conquest of the land.[22] If that was so, it is remarkable that what we now have of the Yahwist's work should conclude without any such climax being reached. H.W. Wolff has made several most illuminating remarks on this fact. To begin with, he points to the quite secondary place that the land occupies in the first of the divine promises, Gen. 12.1-3:

> It appears in an almost unrecognizable form as a dim remembrance in the subordinate clause of verse 1: 'Go ... to the land which I will show you. 'Show!' Here is no longer the solemn promise of the gift of the land as it appears so momentously in 12.7 or 28.13 in the traditional material, whose motto is 'I give'. The theme is reduced to a secondary feature of the narrative.[23]

Secondly, Wolff believes that the conquest material was played down by the Yahwist, so that for all practical purposes he regards the Yahwist's work as coming to an end with its last appearance in the Tetrateuch, viz. in the Balaam narratives. Thirdly, Wolff infers that

> the Yahwist does not yet wish to write the history of the fulfilment of the promise ... That (the families of the earth should find blessing in Israel is something the Yahwist must still put before Israel *as a kerygma* ... [24] Even the Yahwist preaches to a situation 'between promise and fulfilment'.[25]

Does this then not mean, W. Zimmerli asks, that the Yahwist's audience—whom he takes to be the Solomonic generation—are not meant to regard themselves as living in a time of fulfilment of the promise, but to see that 'from here a further waiting and hoping stretches out toward a yet unfulfilled future?'[26]

Interesting though these suggestions are, it seems to me necessary, before ascribing intentions of this kind to the Yahwist, to decide whether or not his work told the story of the conquest of the land. If it did, and especially if it ended on that note, it is impossible to say, as Wolff tries to, that the Yahwist intended at the same time to play down the theme of fulfilment. And if the Yahwist's work originally included the conquest, it must have been only through accident or the design of others in the course of the composition of the Pentateuch that his work came to be foreshortened. It will be to those others—those editors or redactors—that we must attribute the removal of the fulfilment element, and the Yahwist himself cannot be credited with that meaningful truncation.

But if, on the other hand, the Yahwist did originally conclude his history with the oracles of Balaam foreseeing a blessed and dominant future for Israel (Num. 24.15ff.), but left the narrating of Israel's success out of his work and for another time, then we may ascribe to the Yahwist this second element also of the Pentateuch's theme: viz. the promise awaiting fulfilment. For in this case the shape of the Yahwist's work and of the Pentateuch will be in the two major respects identical; both will be carried along by the theme of the divine promise, and both will come to an end on the eve of the fulfilment of that promise.

Perhaps it is too much to hope that we shall ever know—despite the certainty of scholars on each side of the argument—whether or not the Yahwist's narrative included the conquest. Nevertheless, what remains valuable for our purpose from the insights of Wolff is that even if the significance of the non-fulfilment of the promise is wrongly ascribed to the Yahwist, it can be rightly ascribed to the author(s) of the final form of the Pentateuch; for there can be no doubt about where that work ends: with Israel outside the land and the promises yet to be realized.

Deuteronomy also, though for reasons different from the Yahwist's, stands, as von Rad says,

> in the middle between promise and fulfilment. ... In this very condition of 'not yet' [Israel] is threatened by many dangers ... Much can still happen, even disaster. We can even speak of a deep concern which runs through the Deuteronomic paraclesis, that Israel in the last minute before the fulfilment could lose the salvation.[27]

The presence of a book of this character at the end of the Pentateuch serves only to emphasize the open-endedness of the promise which the Yahwist and the Priestly writers in their own way have to make Israel aware of. But these sentences from von Rad, stressing the dangers confronting Israel, are not the sum and substance of this book. While Israel is left in little doubt of the real dangers of disobedience, the thrust of Deuteronomy is positive. For though it begins with the story of Israel's rebellions and acts of faithlessness (e.g. 1.26, 32) it concludes with a farewell speech of encouragement by Moses (31.2-6) and his blessing upon the tribes (ch. 33), to which is appended a note concerning the loyalty Israel will give Joshua (34.9); and throughout the book it is taken for granted that at least the promise of land will be fulfilled (e.g. 31.3, 7, 20). Nevertheless, the certainty of Israel's eventual disobedience (31.16-21, 27ff.) is as firm as that of God's intentions to fulfil his promises; and thus the time between promise and fulfilment is an opportunity for faith.[28]

With the Priestly Work we face at the beginning the same literary-critical problem as we did with the Yahwist: did the work originally include an account of the conquest? Here, unlike the situation with J, it would seem to be generally denied that P extended beyond the Pentateuch.[29] For P, the re-creating moment of conquest lies in the future; it may even be said that the 'key to priestly theology is that the promise of the land of blessing still endures and will be realized soon'.[30] Far from offering merely a legitimation of current cultic practice through its retrojection into the Mosaic past, P looks to the future, not only with a programme for a revived cult but with an assurance that the cult will be revived, and that in the land of promise.

> The story of the events which issue in the gracious approach of God to his people under Moses, is for [the priestly writer] without doubt not only a narrative written in retrospect about an ancient 'once upon a time'. Where God ... condescends to his people and promises himself to this people, we are not dealing with an aorist tense, but rather with a perfect, yes, even with a future perfect.[31]

To whom then do we owe the conclusion of the Pentateuch with Israel on the edge of Jordan, rather than having obtained the land of promise? The narrative of the conquest could easily have formed part of the Pentateuch: for it existed, at the time of the final redaction of the Pentateuch, in the Deuteronomistic History, and it perhaps was included in the Yahwist's work, and possibly also in the Priestly Work. It is impossible to be sure whether the final (priestly) redactor of the Pentateuch stopped where he did because that was a traditional moment of pause in the canonical history, or whether this break was his own creation, designed for the situation of his own time. Why he ended where he did we cannot say, but what it meant to have ended there was of considerable significance, as the next chapter will show.

10

Function

a. Historical

We should finally consider the function of the Pentateuch, given that it is a book with such a theme as has been described above, at the time when it came into existence. (I would rather speak of 'function' than of 'purpose' since one cannot assume that the functions it served were consciously intended by its final author(s), and since we do not have access to the intentions of its writer(s), we can only make reasoned assumptions about the kind of significance or function it is likely to have had in its own time.)

The question of historical function demands an answer to a prior literary-critical question: at what period was the Pentateuch in its final shape[1] brought into being? The answer that has long been popular is that the Pentateuch as a whole (and not only some part of it) provided the basis for Ezra's reform and was probably brought by him from Babylonia,[2] though of course that event is variously dated as 458 or 398 BCE, or some time between those dates. Some have recently called into question this consensus view, alleging that the Ezra narrative is nothing but a piece of 'edificatory "church history"',[3] but this appears to me an unnecessarily sceptical view of the Ezra material, and the evidence that the law invoked by Ezra and Nehemiah contained not only P but also at least J (the Yahwist's work) and D (the Deuteronomist's work)[4] seems conclusive enough to affirm that the Pentateuch was in existence by the end of the fifth century.

If that is the case, and if, as is generally assumed, the redaction of the Pentateuch took place in Babylonia, the crucial point about the historical setting of the Pentateuch is that it is a product of the Babylonian exile. It is customary, indeed, to regard the exile as having reached its end with Cyrus's permission in 539 BCE for the exiles to return (Ezra 1.1-4); but while that may have been the view of the Chronicler and of those exiles who did return, from the standpoint of Jews still in Babylonia in the fifth century, like Ezra and Nehemiah and those who accompanied Ezra on his return to the land (Ezra 7.7; 8.1-20), the exile was still a reality long after 539. The Pentateuch, even if it was composed after 539 BCE, is still an exilic work!

The significance of such a setting is that the Pentateuch functions as an address to exiles, or, perhaps it would be better to say, the self-expression of exiles, who find themselves at the same point as that reached by the Israelite tribes at the end of Deuteronomy: the promise of God stands behind them, the promised land before them. What von Rad says of Deuteronomy is apt also for the Pentateuch as a whole: it 'erases seven centuries of disobedience and thoughtless ingratitude, places Israel once more in the desert before God, and lets Israel hear again the gracious election to be the people of the Lord's possession'.[5]

To be more specific: wherever exilic Jewry opens the Pentateuch it finds itself. Genesis 1–11 is not for them, as it is for us, universal history; it is their own history. Far from being simply a narrative about the nations, a theological portrait of the relationship of God and humanity in general, those chapters are heard in exile as a story of God and Israel. The dispersion of the nations (Gen. 11) is Israel's own diaspora, the flood is the uncreation of Israel's life at the time of the destruction of Jerusalem, and the judgments of God upon primaeval disobedience, murder, lust and hybris are his righteous judgments upon sinful Israel. Yet the movement towards life and salvation that the primeval history manifests is also understood afresh in exile as a word of hope to the exiles. They see in Genesis 1–11 a remnant saved alive out of the disaster of uncreation, they hear in Genesis 8 a divine promise that such a disaster will not recur, and in ch. 11 they find an unbroken line that stretches from the moment of dispersion to the divine summons, 'Go forth ... to the land ...; I will make of you a great nation' (12.1f.).

In the patriarchal narratives, exilic Israel reads not only the lives of its ancestors but also its own life story. To the Jewish exiles, as descendants of Abraham, the divine promises are spoken no less directly than to their forefather. As Jacob-Israel they have spent too many years in Mesopotamia but have heard a voice from Bethel saying, 'I will not leave you until I have done that of which I have spoken to you' (Gen. 28.15) and have found themselves responding, as at the Jabbok, with the determination of one who strives with God and prevails: 'I will not let you go, unless you bless me' (32.26). They dream that their departure into exile was accompanied by the word, 'Do not be afraid to go down to Egypt [read, Babylon]; for I will there make of you a great nation. I will go down with you to Egypt, and I will also bring you up again' (46.3f.). They can even learn to dare to say, like Joseph, of their exile, 'You meant evil against me; but God meant it for good, to bring it about that many people should be kept alive, as they are today' (50.20). And even those who lie dying before the return can take place find themselves taking an oath of their sons, saying, 'God will visit you, and you shall carry up my bones from here' (cf. 50.25).

The bondage in Egypt is their own bondage in Babylon, and the exodus past becomes the exodus that is yet to be. Above all, in the books of Exodus and Leviticus, exilic Israel, in whatever measure it is listening to its Torah, hears anew the divine commands from Sinai, and responds with an 'All that Yahweh has spoken we will do'. The post-exilic community's commitment to the law must be attributed at base to its renewed encounter during the exile with this Pentateuchal theme of the divine–human relationship, promised and partly fulfilled, but still awaiting a fuller realization—in the land. The dangers threatening the fulfilling of the relationship of Yahweh and Israel are vividly re-presented to exilic Israel in the convolutions of the Sinai episodes, while the decision to return to Egypt—which has now taken the shape of a decision to remain in Babylonia—has to be rejected once more by every Israelite family that would be in covenant with Yahweh in the land of promise. And Leviticus, studied in Babylonia by priests and laymen alike, ensures that the renewed worship in the temple will be no bloodless de-ritualized cult but a full restoration of what Israel believes to be its ancestral cult practised since Mosaic times. In the detail of ritual legislation and behavioural prescription Israel reminds itself of what it must mean to be the holy people of Yahweh. The very impossibility of performing the will of God in exile inevitably points Israel towards the future and requires an imaginative projection of themselves into the time when they are resettled—in the land.

Numbers and Deuteronomy, for their part, function among exilic Jewry not primarily as the story of Israel's past life, but as a dream for its future existence. From the census at Sinai to the blessing of Moses, Israel reads a programme of events that now belong not to its past, but to its future. The march across the desert, without ark of the covenant, fire, or cloud, but nonetheless with devoted objects for the temple (cf. Ezra 1.5-11; 8.24-34), will be, as at the first, a divinely led procession.[6] Hostility from non-Jews, Numbers warns by its narrative, is only to be expected, and measures are to be taken to counteract aggression and to ensure the safe arrival of Yahweh's people and his possessions (cf. Ezra 8.21ff.; Neh. 2.7, 9). But beyond a programme and prudential advice, these Pentateuchal books offer the exiles something even more valuable: the exhortation of their most revered leader, Moses. In the speeches of Deuteronomy Israel hears a parenesis without which the permissions of Persian kings may well have been a dead letter; only those whose spirit God had stirred to go up to Jerusalem ever left Babylonia, according to the Chronicler (Ezra 1.5). Beyond doubt the book of Deuteronomy was a vehicle of the divine prompting of Israel to set its face toward the land. The return of Nehemiah to the land was clearly inspired by Deuteronomy, no matter how much self-regarding motives may also have entered into his decision; his prayer that God would see to it that he should be allowed permission to return breathes the spirit of Deuteronomy, Moses' promise of restoration to the land being explicitly referred to (Neh. 1.5-11; cf. Deut. 30.1-5). And Ezra, for his part, is said to have gone up to Jerusalem *because* he had set his heart to study the law of Yahweh and to do it (Ezra 7.7, 10). To study the Pentateuch and to 'do' it leads an exilic Jew ultimately to the land. Nevertheless, even though Deuteronomy ends with the still potent blessing of Moses upon the tribes, and even though it is taken for granted throughout the book that Israel will enter the land, Moses' last speeches have emphasized that even on the brink of fulfilment of this third promise Israel is still open to the possibility of curse as well as of blessing (Deut. 27.11–28.68; 29.2 [Heb. 29.1]–30.19; 31.26-29).

The Pentateuchal theme, in its several forms, functioned among the exiles as an interpretation of their history, a summons to obedience in their present, and a hope that led to action. Literature arising out of a vast array of historical situations had been welded into a new unit with a definite and effective function.

b. Theological

From what has been said above, it is plain that the historical function of the Pentateuch and its theme was primarily a theological one; so there may seem to be a certain arbitrariness in separating the Pentateuch's *historical* function from its *theological*. But, on the other hand, it is one thing to reconstruct the function that the Pentateuchal theme served in its presumed original historical context, and quite another to insist on leaving the Pentateuch encapsulated in its historical context, as if the critic's task were done once the work had been located and explicated within that context. To rest content with its historical significance is to fall prey yet again to the fallacy of the all-sufficiency of the historical-critical method. Indeed, quite apart from the (historical) fact that the Pentateuch *has* had, in the centuries following its origin, all kinds of significances other than its original one(s), it is an abuse of historical criticism to imagine that the significance it posits for the Pentateuch must be the only true significance of the work.

But it is equally an affront to the text to uproot it entirely from its historical origins (in as far as we know what they are) in the interests of enabling it to function in other contexts. The last thing I would want to do to the Pentateuch (or to any other work of ancient literature) would be to 'make it relevant to modern people' or 'update' its message by ignoring its time-conditioned aspect and extracting from it a swarm of free-floating 'timeless truths'. This form of de-naturing the text, familiar to most preachers as the only safe way of letting the Old Testament loose in a Christian congregation, is worse than a return to mediaeval allegorization since it lacks even the theological and hermeneutical rules by which mediaeval exegesis was protected against total subjectivity in interpretation.[7]

Is there a middle way, then, between keeping the Pentateuch firmly encased in the past, on the one hand, and, on the other, so lopping off its historical roots that it becomes merely an *objet trouvé*, a trigger for any reader's subjective reactions? Is there, in other words, any way in which the Pentateuch can be said to have a *contemporary* religious function that respects its *past* religious function? I think so. I suggest two ways—there may well be others—by which the Pentateuch, like other literature, can function in a time beyond its own.

1. Story

The first way begins from the recognition that the Pentateuch is essentially a *narrative*. To suppose that because it is 'torah' it is therefore 'law' is a fatal mistake. It is as much in its story-telling functions as in its explicitly directive commandments that it is 'torah', 'guidance'. The patriarchal narratives are as much 'torah' as are the Ten Commandments, the story of rebellion in the wilderness and the Blessing of Moses no less 'torah' than the levitical sacrificial code. The Pentateuch is, in fact, an outstanding example within world literature of the continually self-renewing function of religious story. As story, it could serve as the paradigm for the interpretation of the bulk of the biblical material, story and not history being the primary mode of communication of religious truth, and story-telling about a God who is already revealed and known rather than revelation from God being the primary character of the Bible's substance.[8] Only the role of poetry in the Biblical corpus is done a disservice by such an analysis; but since we meet with comparatively little poetry in the Pentateuch, we may leave that out of account here.[9]

To understand, then, how the Pentateuch functions as a theological work that transcends its own time of origin, we have to consider the nature of *story.* [10] What is offered in a story is a 'world'—make-believe or real, familiar or unfamiliar. To the degree that the hearer or reader of the story is imaginatively seized by the story, to that degree he or she 'enters' the world of the story. That means that the reader of the story, when powerfully affected by it, becomes a participant of its world. One learns, by familiarity with the story, one's way about its world, until it becomes one's own world too.[11]

The Pentateuch as a story therefore performs the function of creating a 'world' that is to a greater or lesser extent unlike the world of its readers, and that invites its reader to allow the horizons of their own world to merge with those of that other world.[12] And to respond to that invitation is to allow oneself to be worked upon, influenced, by the story—that is, to expose oneself to the possibility of the story becoming one's own story (biography).

Here we may pause to analyse some aspects of the nature of story, and to enquire how the story-quality of the Pentateuch preserves it alive to function as a religious and literary work in our own age.

1. Story highlights the freedom of action enjoyed by humans and gods—which often means the mystery of human or divine action. At the opposite pole from behaviouristic or mechanistic theories of action, story emphasizes the role of the inexplicable and the undetermined.

> No attempt is made in stories to reduce everything to a principle of sufficient reason ... to find a necessary and sufficient cause for every effect ... Stories acknowledge the place of mystery as a natural element in reality. No attempt is made to explain mystery away or relegate it pejoratively to a realm of not-yet discovered knowledge.[13]

The Pentateuch, with its express avowal of the mystery of Israel's election—not for its size or its righteousness but only because of the unconditioned promise to the ancestors (Deut. 07.7f.; 9.4-7)—and its equally firm insistence upon the freedom of human actions—even when they are leading the Hebrew family toward a destiny already divinely determined—[14] is in competition, whenever it is read today as scripture or as literature, with our contemporary congenital 'scientific' outlook so deeply distrustful of mystery. I may warm to the Pentateuchal story's world of mystery and find the eyes of my understanding opened by it to the reality of my own life; or I may pronounce the mystery nothing but mystification and batten down the story of a inexplicable promise that threatens to conquer the world and bring all the families of the earth under its self-styled 'blessing'. But however I respond, the Pentateuchal story will be at work sucking me into its world or else perhaps making it ever clearer that it is a world I have, or wish to have, no part in.

2. Within the story there is no distinction between the real and the unreal. Everything that happens really happens (whether we believe it or not).[15] In the history of western philosophy, reality has tended either to be identified with appearance or to be contrasted with it. Either, as in the empirical tradition, only what is observable is real, or else, as in the Platonic tradition, only the universal is real, and appearance is mere appearance or illusion. But story moves freely in both realms—or rather, refuses to acknowledge that there *are* two realms. We do not put down a comic novel because its plot becomes surrealistic; we do not walk out of the theatre because the play hangs upon improbable coincidences; we do not shun the opera because its actors sing to one another instead of speaking, as people

generally do, or because they take an unconscionably long time dying. We yield ourselves to the reality of story: a suspension of belief, some may call it, but more correctly, perhaps, we should term it a willing suspension of our everyday sets of operational beliefs for the sake of those of the story. This openness to the reality of the story only the most hard-headed—and hard-hearted—will call escapism. There is a coherence, an inner logic, in any well-wrought story that makes for most of us all questions of congruence with the world that we perceive as reality fall away. 'In story', Robert Roth says, 'there is no distinction between nature and supernature, and consequently no hierarchy of values'[16] by which either nature or supernature, however defined, is elevated above the other.

As far as the Pentateuch is concerned, this characteristic of story means that the Pentateuch functions as reality from beginning to end. No awkward historical questions about the material of the Pentateuch stand in the way of its efficacy in creating 'world' or in drawing its readers into participation in its world. Jacob's dream of an encounter at the Jabbok with a heavenly wrestler is as real as the relationship of Joseph and his brothers, which is as real as the bush that burned and was not consumed, which is as real as the exodus from Egypt or the engraving of the tables of stone by the finger of God. (Banquo's ghost is as real as the murder of Duncan.) When we say, This is myth, this is legend, this is history, this is poetry, this is hyperbole, we are not looking at the story as story, but straight through it, at what may be behind it.[17] And when we look through or past the story, it cannot of course function as story. Given half the degree of willing suspension of 'belief' that we exercise every day when we sit before the television screen or pick up a novel, readers of the Pentateuch's story soon come to know the character of life lived in the tension between promise and fulfilment, and the nature of action that is at one and the same time free and predetermined (though they may never come to know whether Abraham was an historical personage nor what precisely happened at the Sea of Reeds).

3. Of all that may be said of story, the most obvious fact is that it moves through time. Though a story will probably, as in the Aristotelian definition of drama (performed story), have a beginning and an end,[18] the third element, its middle, is of unquestionable significance for understanding its essence. For the middle of a story represents reality as in movement. This is a view of reality at odds with most philosophical and many theological outlooks. Only process philosophy and the eschatological strand in theology (represented best in the contemporary period by theologies of 'hope') can be said to share story's fundamental datum, that reality is in motion. Elsewhere in philosophy and theology, ontology (the nature of being rather than of becoming) and explorations of static phenomena have dominated the scene. The development of particle physics has indeed put out of court purely 'fixist' views of reality,[19] but even the constant motion of the subatomic world does not present quite the same view of reality as does story. For the movement of story, unlike the apparently random and only accidentally or occasionally creative motion of particles, is always purposive and goal-oriented. Now while this is obviously true about story, it is not obviously true of reality. A slice of 'life', individual or communal, cut along geographical or temporal lines, usually looks anything but purposive; inasmuch as it is not simply random, the direction of its movement is hard to pinpoint, and the goal of its movement can rarely be discerned. So it is a particular decision about reality, a particular judgement about the shape of human existence, that is presupposed by story. The fact that we allow that there are such things as stories already means that we have decided (or perhaps better, desired) to order the apparent randomness of events into a meaningful sequence. Story creates order out of the flux of happenings by arranging them in (or, discerning in them—let the question remain unresolved) such a chain of connectedness that leads one to speak of the end as the goal and the middle as directed movement.[20] The most elementary analysis of narrative form, into exposition, complication, and resolution further illustrates the goal-directedness of story.

10. Function

If we turn from these observations to the Pentateuch again, its significance as story is readily apparent. Time is its first, not its fourth, dimension. Commencing as it does, not *in medias res* (with a plunge into the whirlpool of reality), nor with the birth of a hero, nor *ab urbe condita* (from the foundation of some city or institution) but with unconditioned 'beginning' (*rē'šît*, Gen. 1.1[21]), and moving through antediluvian lifetimes, through genealogical tables and patriarchal biographies, down to time-scales of forty years and of forty days and until the particular 'this day' of Deuteronomy, the Pentateuch encompasses all time as a sequence that moves inexorably in one direction toward a single goal. And more than most stories, more even than most epics, the Pentateuch refuses to leave the goal unspecified or to allow it to be only gradually unveiled; in the Pentateuch the goal is explicit from the beginning in the promises that call for fulfilment. Especially if Genesis 12 is read as a recapitulation and redefinition of the primal intentions of God for humans (land, descendants, a divine–human relationship), the Pentateuch gives its hand away at its very beginning—not, indeed, to foreshorten the enormous distance between Genesis 1 and Deuteronomy 34 or to dissipate the sense of movement, but precisely to signify that the reality it portrays, of relentless movement toward a goal, is the major significance this vast segment of human history holds.

Most remarkably, from the standpoint of the nature of story, the Pentateuch's determined movement towards a goal is matched only by its failure to reach that goal. It has a beginning and a middle, but no end. True, the death of Moses provides a formal end for the Pentateuch, but this is no hero's death that rounds off the story, and this cannot be the end to which the Pentateuchal promises have been driving. How different the mood of Deuteronomy 34 is from the last lines, let us say, of Milton's *Samson Agonistes:*

> All is best, though we oft doubt,
> What th' unsearchable dispose
> Of highest wisdom brings about,

> And ever best found in the close ...
> His servants he with new acquist
> Of true experience from this great event
> With peace and consolation hath dismiss'd,
> And calm of mind all passion spent.

For the Pentateuch, far from concluding with 'all passion spent', presses beyond itself to a goal that lies still in the future even when its story is over. To the reader of conventionally structured narratives the Pentateuch's conclusion is frustrating. But therein a question about the reader's perception of reality or one's preferred shape of reality is posed: must one have stories that spend themselves in the telling, or can one live with a story that remains incomplete? That question about story may well be a question, or challenge, about life—and not merely about life in general, but about one's own life. The Pentateuch as story confronts us existentially, that is, with a probing of our own existence,

4. The movement of story is often played out in spatial as well as temporal terms. That is to say, more stories than one might think are 'travel' stories. The *Odyssey* is an ancient example, but not the most ancient: the Sumerian *Gilgamesh* is already a deeply symbolic representation of a view of man as a traveller, as *homo viator*, the human voyager, to use the title of a collection of essays by Gabriel Marcel.[22] Paul Zweig even claims that the adventure story—which generally is a travel story—is the oldest, most persistent subject matter of story in the world, and that adventure is 'constitutive of culture itself'.[23] John Navone boldly characterizes the Bible as a whole as 'a book of travel stories about God and his "chosen ones"'.[24]

What does it signify about our view of reality that we so frequently cast our stories in the form of travel stories? We cannot airily dismiss this form as a merely literary or narrative 'device', such as enables the protagonists of the story to be portrayed in successively differing situations and in differing sets of relationships. Something deeper about our view of humanity is implied by our cultural inheritance of travel stories and our continuing creation of them. Let me suggest that our love of travel stories springs from the desire of the unsettled to be settled, and of the settled to be unsettled. That is, the rootless identify with the travellers who search for a home, and the secure identify with the travellers who leave home. The human reality at the core of this twofold desire is not simple dissatisfaction with the ways things are, whether on the part of the settled or of the unsettled, but an expression of a tension within the unsettled and the settled to be both—to encompass both experiences. In commonplace shape settled suburbanites, for example, recognize this dialectic in their experience of vacations: they long to be away from home and from the routine of everyday life, and yet they are always glad to be back—not because they cannot make up their minds whether they would rather be at home or away, but because they want to experience both rootedness and uprootedness. They sense that both experiences are important for a realization of their human potentiality. In less familiar shape we know of the unsettled (seminomads, gypsies, tramps, explorers) who long for a place but are glad to be on the road. Few humans are wholly settled or wholly rootless; our perception of our existence as partly the one, partly the other is—if we have come to recognize such a perception in ourselves—a matter of choice, largely subconscious perhaps, but nonetheless a choice. It is a particular and not a self-evident analysis of the human condition, or, nearer to home, so to speak, of our own biographies. Our entanglement with travel stories, if we know that experience, bespeaks both our perception and our wish: that we have it and want to have it both ways, to be running away and to be headed towards.[25]

What then of the Pentateuch? Here everyone seems constantly on the move. The longest period of stasis in the narrative of the Pentateuch is passed over in one chapter (Exodus 1). Otherwise, if we allow ourselves to travel with the story, we journey from Ur to Canaan, from Canaan to Upper Mesopotamia and back again, from Canaan to Egypt five times (with Abraham, Joseph, twice with the sons of Jacob, with Jacob and his family) and from Egypt to Canaan four times—to say nothing of the journeying outward that begins already in Genesis 3 towards the east of Eden, that continues in Genesis 4 with exile to the land of travelling ('Nod'), and that engages the whole human race in Genesis 11 as people, in migrating from the east, are further projected into travelling by being scattered abroad over the face of all the earth (11.2, 8f.). Even when the chief actors in the narrative are comparatively settled, movement persists. Abram comes to the land of Canaan (Gen. 12.5), but thereafter is found 'passing through' the land (12.6), 'removing' from one place to another within the land (12.8), 'journeying on' (12.9; 13.3), 'walking through the length and breadth of the land' (13.17), 'moving his tent' (13.18), 'journeying toward the south' (20.1), 'going to the land of Moriah' (22.2).

Move into the remainder of the Pentateuch (strange how the idiom of travel adapts so well to the analysis of story!), and we find that Exodus to Deuteronomy is nothing else but the travel story of Israel from Egypt to Canaan. Hardly has Exodus begun than Yahweh announces that he has 'come down to deliver [my people] from the hand of the Egyptians, and to bring them up from that land into a good and broad land, into a land flowing with milk and honey' (3.8). Thereafter the story of the Pentateuch can be told as a traveller's tale: the preparations for departure, the hazards of departure, privations and dangers on the journey, decisions to go back and to move on, moments of rest and days of march, failure to reach the goal even when it is within sight, years of fruitless wanderings and encampments, experiences of pitched battles and dissensions within the company, of deaths and miraculous escapes.

But the journey, what is it? Is it a *nostos*, a homecoming, tortuous and wearisome and rich in experience, like that of Odysseus:

> Many cities of humans he saw and learned their mind, and many were the woes in his heart he suffered on the sea, striving for his life and the homecoming of his comrades.[26]

His is a return to a home that will certainly not be the home that was left decades ago but that will nevertheless be 'home'? Israel's homecoming will be like his, for the land to which they travel is the land of their ancestors (Gen. 48.21; cf. 31.3), the land of the Hebrews (Gen. 40.15), the land where their forebears have dwelt. But it is a home that the generation of the exodus has never seen for themselves; it is 'home' as third-generation expatriates in a British colony would refer, not twenty years ago, to England as their home though they lived their whole life on the other side of the globe. More, the journeying is a homecoming only for two individuals out of all those who left Egypt (Caleb and Joshua: Num. 14.22ff.; 26.65; 32.12; Deut. 1.36). Unlike Odysseus, there is no hero in this tale who survives, against all odds, the rigours of the *nostos,* losing his men left, right and centre on the way; in this tale the only candidate for hero-hood fails to achieve a *nostos,* while the homecoming of the two second-rankers pales into insignificance beside the meaning of the return for the company as a whole. And even so, the land to which Israel returns is a land that has never really been their own. 'Land of the ancestors' it may be called once or twice, but overwhelmingly it is 'the land of the Canaanites' (e.g. Deut. 1.7), the land that has only been *promised* to Abraham and his descendants, the land in which the ancestors have lived as sojourners, the land that at the return will have to be fought for as if it had never been Israel's at all. Odysseus may have to dispose of the suitors upon his return, but at least Penelope is still there, intact. Israel has no stake in the land that is its destination, nothing to call its own when it arrives.

Then if the journey is not foremost a homecoming, is it, like that of the Roman ancestor Aeneas, a laborious *search* for a new home, a home away from home, a homeland where a new race may grow?

> Long labours, both by sea and land, he bore,
> And in the doubtful war, before he won
> The Latian realm, and built the destined town.[27]

Yes, up to a point, and, as with Aeneas's journey, a divine destiny leads Israel's march on to *the* place in which Israel may spread its wings and become a great people in the course of many generations. But Israel, unlike Virgil, tells its primal travel story not as a tale of an abandonment of home under the divine impulse to search out a new home, nor as the rejection, in obedience to the divine command, of some alluring potential home other than the place dictated by the divine destiny *(Aeneid,* Book IV)—but as the story of an *escape* from a home that was not a home in order to make for a home that had never been a home. Israel were 'sojourners', and so truly homeless, in Egypt (Exod. 22.21 [Heb. 22.20]; Deut. 10.19) just as much as their ancestors had been 'sojourners' in the land of the Canaanites and the Hittites (Gen. 23.4; 35.27). They are the unsettled in pursuit of the unobtained.

Now whether or not it is an accident of literary history that has allowed the Pentateuch to conclude without the goal of Israel's journey being reached, it is fundamental for the interpretation of the Pentateuch that it ends where it does, and basic for an understanding of it as a travel story to recognize it as a very peculiar tale of travel. It neither starts from home nor arrives at home. By no means does it appeal to the human longing to 'run away from home', to be on the loose, to cut one's ties with the past, to explore, to follow one's fancy; for the journey in the Pentateuch is unavoidably towards a definite, explicit place, and the travellers on that journey, far from cutting themselves off from the past, carry with them a heavy freight of memory—as well as Joseph's bones (Gen. 50.25; Exod. 13.19)! By no means either does the Pentateuchal journey match the human desire for rootedness, for it is told in a tale of abandonment of security (cf. Exod. 16.3; Num. 11.4ff.) in exchange for insecurity, a tale which—inasmuch as it is not a story of failure to reach the goal—presents the goal as struggle before rest (e.g. Deut. 3.18ff.), as a place of potential curse as well as blessing (Deut. 11.26-32), as a land that can be lost (Deut. 28.63f., 68) as well as won. Who wants to travel that road? Would it not be better, after all, to stay in Egypt, even perhaps in Haran?

Who wants, in short, to view one's own life as neither moving in towards a comfortable homecoming nor moving out towards heroic adventure? Who among the rootless wants to identify with travellers who do not reach their goal? Who among the secure can identify with travellers leaving a place that is not home? The Pentateuch offers us an unattractive option for our self-understanding, that jibes none too well with our habitual perceptions. It offers us a world where 'you never reach the promised land; you only march toward it', as a British Prime Minister once said. But you do not win elections with such a slogan; you even make the most percipient self-critic edgy.

2. Promise

The theme of the Pentateuch, I have been suggesting, functions for times other than its own through being cast in the form of a story, and of a particular kind of story at that. Now I want to try a different tack, and argue that it also functions as (religious) literature through its central conceptual content: promise, or rather, divine promise, or rather still, divine promise awaiting fulfilment.

A few pages in Jürgen Moltmann's *Theology of Hope*,[28] dependent in many ways upon Walther Zimmerli's famous essay on 'Promise and Fulfillment',[29] say almost all that needs to be said by way of analysis of the concept of promise. I propose to do little more than take up some of his points and apply them to the Pentateuchal theme.

1. A promise binds humans to the future. Such a future is 'not the vague goal of possible change; it is not openness towards coming events as such'.[30] 'Whatever will be will be' is an attitude of openness to the future, but only to an indeterminate and unknown future; it is poles apart from a promise that directs towards a specific future. Hartshorne has defined the future as the indeterminate, as distinct from the past that is the determinate and the present that is in process of becoming determinate.

Even if the indeterminateness of the future were to be reckoned as merely a token of our ignorance[31] (that is, even if the future were already determined, and its indeterminateness should be only appearance), such a future would be a future without a promise. Promise and fate cannot coexist.

In the Pentateuch Israel is bound to a future that has been *promised* to them: though the progeny faces extinction, though the divine–human relationship threatens to fall apart, though the land evades them, there is no question but that Israel is intelligible only in terms of its future. If to be human is to be *unterwegs,* 'on the way', as Ernst Bloch has it, to be Israel is to be pre-eminently so, according to the Pentateuchal story.

2. Promise is more than hope. To say that is in no way to denigrate hope, to class it with the deceptiveness of hope (*elpis*) as attested in Greek literature. For Theognis, for example, 'Hope and danger are alike; both are evil genies'.[32] For Sophocles, hope is at least ambivalent or ambiguous: 'Deceitful (*polyplangktos*) hope brings profit to many, but to many it proves only the mockery of their thoughtless desires'.[33] For many writers, a distinction had to be made between good hope (*elpis agathē*) and bad, deceptive hope (*elpis kakē*).[34]

These are not peculiarly Greek views, of course. Pascal could lament hope as a distraction from the realities of the present:

> We are never satisfied with the present ... We scarcely ever think of the present; if we do it is only to obtain light wherewith to organize the future. The present is never our goal; the past and present are our means; the future alone is our objective. Thus we never live, but only hope to live; and as we are for ever preparing to be happy, we shall assuredly never be so.[35]

Pope could observe wryly:

> Hope springs eternal in the human breast;
> Man never is, but always will be blest.[36]

With Goethe, the supreme value of the present outweighs hopes for the future: 'If only the eternal remains present to us every moment, then we do not suffer from the transience of time'.[37]

No, we can view hope infinitely more positively than such writers, and find with Ernst Bloch the principle of hope[38] to be the kernel of human existence. 'Bloch has taught us about the overwhelming power of the still-open future and of the hope that reaches out to it in anticipation', writes Wolfhart Pannenberg.[39] And Moltmann: 'As scarcely any other philosophy *Das Prinzip Hoffnung* is suited to assist in activating and elaborating the Christian doctrine of hope'.[40] Nonetheless, even Bloch's insistence on the power of the future is ultimately a faith in the transcendent quality of hope to reveal humanity as it is yet to be: the religious dimension of hope lies in the significance not of the *Deus absconditus* but of a *homo absconditus,* a being whose potentiality is still latent. Even Bloch can speak almost romantically and certainly wishfully, of hope: 'If it remains strong enough, if it is pure and undistinctly aware of itself, hope will not fail us'.[41]

Does not promise transcend such hope? For such hope we have Bloch's word—and it is a powerful and vibrant word; but for the *promise* the Israel of the Pentateuch believed it had the word of the God of the ancestors.

Walther Zimmerli writes in the concluding chapter of his survey of *Man and His Hope in the Old Testament* that throughout the Old Testament

> it became clear that it was precisely where man was led to the edge of human hopelessness that every look turned away from man and his immanent possibilities. There was at no place a 'principle of hope' that was generally held or believed by man, no existential hope to be discovered in the existential understanding of man or in his understanding of the world. Rather it became clear that it was precisely where the sharpest criticisms of hope were loudest, that man in a frightening recklessness threw himself upon the one he was conscious of as coming to his people.[42]

For the Pentateuch especially, it is divine promise and not mere hope that creates and sustains its momentum.

3. A divine promise 'indicates that the expected future does not have to develop within the framework of the possibilities inherent in the present, but arises from that which is possible to the God of the promise'.[43] Hope itself assumes the possibility of radical change from the present: 'Hope assumes that freedom exists: freedom to become what one now is not, freedom to change not only the course of one's life, but the course of the social history of which one is a part'.[44] But the divine promise goes further, and assures what hope assumes. The Pentateuchal promise is laughable at the time of its first utterances, given the 'possibilities inherent in the present': a progeny for a man 'as good as dead'; a homeland for a man who leaves his home 'not knowing where he was going'; a readiness to offer up the son of whom it had been said, 'Through Isaac shall your descendants be named'; an escape from Egypt 'not fearing the wrath of the king, but enduring as seeing the Invisible One'; a crossing of the sea 'as if on dry land'—to mention only the allusions of Hebrews 11 (vv. 12, 8, 17f., 27, 29). The future in the Pentateuch arises, as Moltmann puts it, 'out of that which is possible to the God of the promise', or, to use the language of Hebrews: 'What is seen is made out of things that do not appear' (11.3). Those who live toward the fulfilment of promise are not seized by a 'passion for the possible', to use Kierkegaard's phrase,[45] but by a passion for the impossible.

One of the distinguishing features of hope, indeed what is claimed to be its 'most important characteristic' psychologically speaking, is that it is *realistic*: 'it seeks, directs itself to, strives for, imagines, and finds the real'.[46] This is what distinguishes it from mere desire, wishing and fantasy. Hope cuts desire and fantasy down to size by confronting them with the actual world of possibilities. At the same time it creates the possibility of achieving goals, for without hope as a sense of what is achievable despair, anxiety and depression set in.[47] Such hope has to be learned through experience. 'One must learn the conditions of objective possibility—the limits of possibility imposed by the structure of reality—as well as the limits of subjective possibility ... The real strength of hope is found in its capacity to set and acknowledge its own limits.'[48] That may indeed be so, but it makes literally a world of a difference whether or not God appears within 'the structure of reality'. The promise indicates, as Moltmann said, that the hoped-for future 'arises from that which is possible to the God of the promise', and not from 'the framework of the possibilities inherent in the present'.[49]

4. The promise creates a sense for history. If it binds humans to the future, it also binds them to the past. 'It does not give [humanity] a sense for world history in general', Moltmann writes, 'nor yet for the historic character of human existence as such, but it binds him to its own peculiar history.'[50] 'Anyone who knows of promise and fulfillment', says Zimmerli, 'is responsible to a yesterday about which he has heard something, and he walks toward a tomorrow.'[51] Israel knows of the land to which it is moving throughout the Pentateuch as a land sworn to the ancestors. Without the assurance of a divine word that comes to them out of the past, their hopes for the future could be merely wishful thinking. Yahweh also is bound by the promise from the past and allows that to control *his* future (cf. e.g. Exod. 32.10, 13).

Hope that springs from promise does not therefore lose touch with the past as its appetite for the future grows. A theology of promise thus distinguishes itself from the new sensibility of hope as J.B. Metz, for example, describes it:

> The relationship to the past takes on more and more a purely aesthetic, romantic or archaic character or it depends on a purely historical interest which simply confirms that the past is over and done with. This modern consciousness has a purely historical relationship to the past, but an existential relation to the future. It frees man from a tyranny of history concerned only with origins, and turns him toward a history conceived with ends.[52]

The Israel of the Pentateuch knows no 'tyranny of history'. It lives out of its past, toward its future. It knows no future that does not arise from its past, that is, from its past as the arena of its encounter with the divine promise. Thus the significance of promise arising out of the past and driving toward the future, cannot be reduced to the present moment. A theology of promise or hope cannot be accommodated within a purely existentialist theology.[53] If every moment is the future in which there is decisive judgment, 'the present ceases to be means to some end and becomes its own end'.[54] Zimmerli writes trenchantly:

> This category [promise/fulfilment] guards against every flight into a timeless, mystical understanding of God's nearness, as well as against an understanding of encounter with God reduced to a single existentialistic point without historical relatedness ... This category is an unlimited safeguard against every attempt at self-redemption from this temporally extending course of history, subject as it is to the lowliness of ever-recurring accidental and unfathomable events.[55]

The Pentateuch thus does not admit of a purely existentialist reading, however deeply it probes the character of human existence and however sharply it challenges the reader existentially. The theme of the Pentateuch is entirely concerned with a future bound to a past out of which the present lives. If Deuteronomy sets before Israel 'this day' life and good, death and evil (30.15), it does not call Israel to an existential decision concerning the immediate future only; it poses the question of Israel's long-term future in terms faithfulness to the past and its promises: 'Choose life, that you and your descendants may live, loving Yahweh your God, obeying his voice, and cleaving to him; for that means life to you and length of days, so that you may dwell in the land that Yahweh swore to your fathers—to Abraham, to Isaac, and to Jacob—to give them' (30.19f.)

5. Since promise always leads into a history, and speaks of what is not now but is only yet to be, the interval between the promise and its redemption is one of tension. In it humans have 'a peculiar area of freedom to obey or disobey, to be hopeful or

resigned'.[56] 'The faith and the love and the hope are all in the waiting' (T.S. Eliot). So long as the promise remains simply a promise, there is room for a 'psychopathology of hope',[57] for abandonment of the promise as a living memory, for hopelessness or for the active attempt to opt out of the society to which the promise belongs. The Pentateuchal epic knows well the tension and distress of waiting for the fulfilment. No one emerges from living along with the Pentateuch's story with any illusions about the joy of hope: the promise can weigh one down with frustration, fear and doubt when it is long in arriving at fulfilment.

And yet, since the focus of expectation is not the promise itself, but the God who promises, there is a certainty: behind the promise 'there stands not a momentary impulse of Yahweh, which can be reversed capriciously tomorrow, on a new impulse; what happens to Israel is that which Yahweh has promised of old in his word'.[58] What is more, God being God, 'the fulfilments can very well contain an element of newness and surprise over against the promise as it was received'.[59] The promises may not be fulfilled according to the letter, but beyond the letter. To live under the Pentateuchal promise is to be assured of becoming a 'great' nation; but will its 'greatness' consist solely in its numerical strength? It is to have the promise of a divine–human relationship; but will that relationship consist in divine directions from Sinai and loyal oaths on Israel's part, or will it lead to the experience of a Job or a Jeremiah? It is to be heir to the promise of land; but is that land to be Canaan, or the land from the River to the Sea, or Judaea, or not solely the land itself as soil but the land as precondition for Israel's history and destiny, the land as the setting for the sacred places of encounter with the divine?

6. In the divine promises of the Old Testament, because the God of the promises is greater than any fulfilment that can be expected, 'in every fulfilment the promise, and what is contained in it, does not yet become wholly congruent with reality and thus there always remains an overspill'.[60] The fulfilments that the Pentateuchal promise looks forward to will not fulfil the

promise 'in the sense that they liquidate it like a cheque that is cashed and lock it away among the documents of a glorious past. The "fulfilments" are taken as expositions, confirmations and expansions of the promise.' Therefore it is not surprising that the partial fulfilments of the triple promise that occur within the Pentateuch have an anticipatory as well as a conclusive function. The divine promise must constantly 'overspill' history because of the inexhaustibility of the God of promise, 'who never exhausts himself in any historic reality, but comes "to rest" only in a reality that wholly corresponds to him'.[61] The Pentateuchal theme, viewed formally as 'story' and conceptually as 'promise', is capable of provoking yet further and deeper insights. Literary works of art, as a recent editor of Sophocles' *Electra* writes, 'have a kind of built-in ambiguity [perhaps we should say, polyvalence], being not so much imitations of life as sources of life, producing fresh intimations in each new reader'.[62] The Pentateuch becomes such a source of life, not by being fed through some hermeneutical machine that prints out contemporary answers to contemporary questions, but through the reader's patient engagement with the text and openness to being seized, challenged, or threatened by the 'world' it lays bare.

11

Afterword

I am writing this Afterword twenty years, to the month, after this book was first conceived. At that time, I had been teaching a course on the Pentateuch at Fuller Theological Seminary in Pasadena, California, four hours a week for twelve weeks or so. I had dealt with all the conventional matters of Pentateuchal criticism, and not a few of the more unconventional. So my class had studied the source analysis of the Flood story, the kerygma of the Yahwist and the theology of Deuteronomy, form criticism, rhetorical criticism, and so on. But what I realized, on the night before my very last class, was that despite all these interesting and intensive studies, we had never tried to see the Pentateuch as a whole, or to say what we thought it was all about. Should not that be the topic of the last class? I fell asleep worrying about what I would do in the morning at 9. When I woke, early, I knew what I wanted to do, and it was really very easy. I wrote the outline for the class, which became the outline for this book. It was simply that (1) the Pentateuch was about the fulfilment—and the non-fulfilment—of the promise it contains, and it was that (2) the promise in the Pentateuch is a threefold one—of descendants, of a divine–human relationship, and of land, and it was that (3) the first of these promises is the primary theme of Genesis, the second of Exodus and Leviticus, and the third of Numbers and Deuteronomy.

Twenty years after that time, I still think they were good insights, and I stand by most of what I wrote in the book. But it should not be very surprising if after such a period I should now want to distance myself somewhat from the book, try to locate it within the climate of scholarship at that time, and want to say how my mind has changed, and what new angles of vision have opened up to me over the intervening years.

a. The Genre of *The Theme of the Pentateuch*

What I realize now, though I could not have recognized it at the time, is that *The Theme of the Pentateuch* is a hybrid of rhetorical criticism and biblical theology. From the newly developing movement of rhetorical criticism I had been encouraged in my belief that there was something missing in the traditional concerns of biblical scholarship with the history and origins of the biblical literature. I wanted to believe that the Bible would benefit from being read as literature, and that the kinds of issues that were raised in general literature should also be posed to the Bible. So, rather than thinking about sources and the historical purpose of the Pentateuch, I asked about its theme and its plot. Some thought this interest in the narrative structure of the Pentateuch was akin to structuralism,[1] but there was no structuralist motivation here. My formation for this book was wholly the theory of literature that was available in the early 70s. And the bulk of the book could be called an early exercise in narratology, regarding the Pentateuch as essentially a narrative and fastening as it did upon the elements of plot in the work.

One of the key features of literary criticism of the 1960s and 1970s was the emphasis on ambiguity and irony.[2] While *The Theme of the Pentateuch* did not explicitly bring these terms to the fore, at least not to the extent that my former colleague David Gunn was doing in his *The Story of King David* and *The Fate of King Saul*,[3] I see now that there was a deep irony in my paradoxical analysis of the theme of the Pentateuch as the fulfilment *and also* the non-fulfilment of the promises. How could the theme of a work be both one thing and its opposite? What kind of formulation would enable two contradictory statements of theme to appear as if they formed one single theme? I notice that I was writing that the theme of the Pentateuch as a whole is 'the partial fulfilment—which implies also the partial non-fulfilment—of the promise to or blessing of the patriarchs' (p. 30), but I could not utter such a paradoxical sentence these days without blushing—or at least embarking immediately upon a deconstructive analysis.

All in all, though, the book as a whole was clearly an early example of literary studies of the Bible. Since it had few precursors, it was necessarily rather defensive, especially in its early pages, about the project in which it was engaged. These days, it is no longer necessary to justify reading the final form of the text or to relegate historical questions to a later chapter (which I did) or to omit them altogether (which I did not). These days there are plenty of literary studies that do not apologize for what they are doing, but simply get on with it.

I think, however, that *The Theme of the Pentateuch* is something of an exception among literary studies in its very strong concentration at the same time upon theology. For it is as much an example of the genre of biblical theology as of literary criticism. If there was an impulse to treat the Pentateuch as a work of literature and to understand it as narrative with a plot and a theme, there was equally an impulse to say how the Pentateuch, thus understood, was also a work of theological value. I believed, in fact, that the traditional concentration on questions of sources and historical setting had marginalized the theology of the Pentateuch, and I came to feel that there was a very close connection between the theme of the Pentateuch expressed literarily and the theme of the Pentateuch expressed theologically. The link between the two was the concept of 'story', which was then much in vogue among theologians.

'Biblical theology' has acquired something of a bad name since the 1970s. Even in 1976 James Barr was saying that the biblical theology movement belonged to the past history of biblical studies.[4] I find it very hard to see what the problem was, except that many exponents of biblical theology were rather uncritical in drawing no distinction between what the Bible said, or was alleged to have said, and what was reasonable for us in a very different age to believe. Some had urged that modern believers should 'think biblically', using the thought categories of ancient Israelites instead of twentieth-century people, as if that were possible, or as if the writing of the Bible in a particular culture validated the thought patterns of that culture for all people of all time. Others had used their own reconstructions of the theology of the Bible to impose certain beliefs upon others as authoritative and divinely inspired. Such views were extreme examples of biblical theology; biblical theology itself seems to me still a perfectly acceptable enterprise if it means an exposition of what the Bible (or parts of it, like the Pentateuch) says on theological matters, or even if it includes a recommendation to people of our time to adopt theological ideas expressed in the Bible.

Inasmuch as *The Theme of the Pentateuch* is an example of biblical theology, especially in its last chapter on the theological function of the Pentateuch, I am not ashamed of it. I do think that I wrongly collapsed the distinction between what the Pentateuch says on the one hand and what on the other hand I would have liked to believe and urge others to believe. Today I would take a more quizzical line about the theology of the Bible, as I will say in more detail below. But the process of reading the Bible in order to develop one's own theological position is a very reasonable one for religious believers of various traditions, so long of course as they do not claim that their readings are normative and beyond challenge. That was not the case with *The Theme of the Pentateuch,* I hope; its theological proposals were meant to be suggestive rather than normative.

b. The Modern and the Postmodern

A key difference between *The Theme of the Pentateuch* and any book I would write on the Pentateuch now can be described as the difference between the modern and the postmodern. I mean by the modern the period since the Enlightenment, when, in a word, rationality became enthroned over dogma. *The Theme of the Pentateuch* exemplifies the interests of the modern period, in which texts have unity and determinate meaning, and in which texts are to be viewed as the expression of their author's consciousness.

Today, since I think that we have moved into a postmodern age,[5] I would be much more careful in speaking of meaning. I would not now be speaking of '*the* meaning' of the Pentateuch nor claiming that 'theme encapsulates the meaning of the work' (p. 24), as if there was only one meaning for the Pentateuch. Nowadays I tend rather to believe that texts do not have meaning in themselves, and that what we call meaning is something that comes into being at the meeting point of text and reader. If that is so, then meaning is reader-dependent and reader-specific, and there are in principle as many meanings as there are readers. This is really no more than what we commonly say when we confess that 'it doesn't mean that for me'—allowing that the same words may have different meanings for different readers. But making it into a theory of meaning and integrating it into our interpretational praxis moves us out of the modern world, where texts have meanings, into the postmodern world, where the meaning of meaning is decidedly problematic.

I notice that *The Theme of the Pentateuch* already had taken a first step away from the conventional modern view of meaning. I had spoken about the 'hermeneutical circle of interaction between text and interpreter', by which I meant a process of readjusting orientation to a literary work that makes the reader 'gradually re-formed by the work itself' (p. 21). Meaning was therefore not a simple graspable object, but something in a certain flux. And the location of meaning was not being sought solely in the text itself, but in an interaction between the reader or interpreter and the text. All the same, I was thinking of the text itself as something fixed, of meaning as essentially residing in the text, and of the reader as making ever-shifting constructions of its meaning. Now, on the other hand, I would want to foreground the reader rather more, or, I should say, readers, since there is no determinate reader any more than there is a determinate text. It is not that these readers are all doing their best to find the meaning embedded in a fixed text, but that the text itself is relative to the readers themselves and is in a way created and recreated in the process of their reading of it. I am tempted to maintain that there is no text without readers—that is, nothing that can meaningfully be called text. It is a similar question whether there can be sound without hearers.

Now, if a text does not have a determinate meaning, it cannot have a 'theme'—not one theme, not just one theme. So I could not now write a book entitled *The Theme of the Pentateuch*. More recently, I have been writing sentences like this:

> Above all, the Pentateuch is a novel in that it is a machine for generating interpretations, to use Umberto Eco's phrase. There are so many complex strands in it, so many fragmentary glimpses of its personalities, that we cannot reduce it to a single coherent graspable unity that all readers will agree upon.[6]

Obviously, such a statement does not square with the claim implied in the title of this book. I now think that there is more than one way of saying 'what the Pentateuch is all about', though I still think that the theme of the fulfilment and non-fulfilment of the threefold promise is *one* fruitful way of talking about the Pentateuch.

Further, if the Pentateuch does not have a determinate meaning or theme, and if its meanings are the creations of its readers, or, let us say, 'what it means to them', the idea of 'legitimate' meanings, which I referred to on p. 21 of the first edition, also becomes problematic. Who is to say, I would now ask, what meanings are and are not 'legitimate'? I myself will of course resist any interpretation that I myself cannot hold or cannot in some way adapt to my own interpretation; but I feel now that I have to accept that my interpretations are relative to myself, and I cannot rule out those of others as being 'illegitimate'. That does not mean for a moment that I think all readings are equally good, or that I cannot develop a better interpretation from hearing someone else's, or that it is a waste of time to try to persuade other people of my interpretation. It is a matter of fact that debates about interpretation do go on, and that people often do change their minds about the interpretation they will adopt. But in the end, the interpretation that we hold to will be the one we ourselves judge to be right or the best; and so will everyone else's. No one can judge for us, and no one can say in a postmodern age that some interpretations are 'legitimate' and others 'illegitimate'.

Finally, the postmodern turn has put an end to the 'modern' idea that the meaning of a text is the meaning intended by the author. That is no doubt the common-sense understanding of meaning, and it is constantly being reinforced whenever we act as authors, saying what we mean and intending to say what we mean and being annoyed if people hearing or reading us do not get the message we intended to mean. Indeed, for many kinds of everyday communication we can manage quite well on the assumption that words and sentences and texts contain the meanings their authors intended to put into them. But on a more theoretical plane, it becomes more and more evident that texts have a life of their own, regardless of what their authors intended by them, and that—more to the point—if readers are making meaning from the texts they encounter, the idea of responsibility to the author, who is in many cases unknown or even unknowable, and to that author's intention, of which perhaps the author personally had only a vague knowledge, fades away. In a postmodern world, we have come to see that reading and interpretation are far more problematic activities than I for one imagined in the 1970s.

c. New Movements in Biblical Criticism

The last two decades have been especially exciting and creative times in biblical scholarship, and it is not surprising that *The Theme of the Pentateuch,* first published in 1978, does not reflect the concerns of 1996. I would identify here just two sets of issues that, from today's perspective, are lacking from the book:

gender and politics.

1. Rightly or wrongly, I date the first inroad of feminism into biblical studies to the 1974 article of Phyllis Trible, 'Depatriarchalizing in Biblical Interpretation'.[7] Though she had attempted a feminist reading of Genesis 2–3 in that article, no one in the 1970s had thought of what a feminist interpretation of the Pentateuch as a whole might look like, and I do not particularly blame myself that I never considered undertaking such an interpretation in my book. But by now we have seen such a wealth of feminist biblical criticism that it would be unthinkable today to write a book on such a large stretch of the biblical literature as the Pentateuch without once explicitly raising feminist questions. I can easily see now, for example, that one of the central concerns of the book, the promise of posterity, has a distinct feminist angle to it. When I wrote the book, descendants were something men had. I was of course just following the drift of the text, which always spoke of Abraham and his 'seed'—screening out the mothers (and their ova) who were equally involved in producing offspring for the patriarchal family. I spoke always of the patriarchs even when I should have been giving voice to the matriarchs.

In editing the book, I have tried to make some verbal amends, but the mindset of the book, as of the Pentateuch itself, is still undeniably male. Not a lot of restitution can be made by writing, for example, 'ancestors' instead of 'patriarchs'—in fact, that may even make things worse. For what must not, and cannot, be hidden is that the biblical text massively and systematically marginalizes women, even in areas of life where they were equally important or even more important than men. And what is not sufficiently appreciated, even today, is that even when we read Pentateuchal stories about women, sometimes powerful and interesting women, we are only ever reading men's stories about women.[8] We are always at a further remove from the women personalities of the Pentateuch than we are from the men, and women readers of our own time are perhaps doubly disadvantaged by the unacknowledged male telling of the story; for they are not only obliged to hear of Pentateuchal women from male storytellers (as everyone is), but they must also to some degree suppress their instinct to read as women since it is to men and not to women that the Pentateuch addresses itself.

What is more, the gender issue has become broader in scope. It is now not just the omission and marginalization of women that must concern us, but the positive projections of male interests and assumptions that must be identified. Someone sometime will have to write on masculinity in the Pentateuch, asking what the Pentateuch has to say to men, as men, and what reading the Pentateuch does to men.[9] It would be a very interesting undertaking to consider, for example, how far the enormous desire the Pentateuch exhibits for a posterity, and especially a distant posterity, is a specifically male interest. To what extent also is the configuration of the divine–human relationship in the Pentateuch a male construction, and how differently would promising and law-giving and covenant-making appear in a world that was not almost exclusively a man's world?

2. The political dimension of the Pentateuch is another aspect that is largely ignored in the present book. In the spirit of the literary criticism of the 1970s, I was regarding the Pentateuch as a 'literary work of art'. That was something of a novelty then, since it focused on the coherence of the text rather than its potential for fragmentation into sources, on the text in its final form rather than the processes of its formation from traditions oral and written, and on the conceptual significance of the work as a whole rather than the meanings of its parts. All that was in order to release the Pentateuch from being locked into the circumstances of its historical setting. But, I have now to confess, it was also one-sided, for the Pentateuch does come from some point or other in history and from some social and political circumstance; even if we do not know much about those settings, our interpretation of the Pentateuch has to be influenced by our recognition that there were such settings, and we had better not think we have finished our business with the Pentateuch until

we have done our best to reconstruct them. Such a line of thinking has become an important thread in biblical criticism of the last two decades, as scholars become increasingly aware of the social and political dimensions and functions of the texts they used to write about more as literary and theological works.[10]

Of course, in undertaking to write on the *theme* of the Pentateuch, I was explicitly ignoring other considerations, and there is no fault in doing only one thing at a time. All I would say now is that if I were writing a book about the Pentateuch from scratch today, I could not write about it simply as a literary work of art. As a matter of fact, even the first edition of *The Theme of the Pentateuch* did not treat it as *solely* a literary work. In Chapter 10, I made some suggestions for the *function* of the work in its own time: I said that the Pentateuch 'functions as an address to exiles, or, perhaps it would be better to say, the self-expression of exiles, who find themselves at the same point as that reached by the Israelite tribes at the end of Deuteronomy: the promise of God stands behind them, the promised land before them' (p. 104). But I did not distinguish between exiles and exiles, I did not wonder which exiles were wanting to convince which other exiles of the truth of the Pentateuch, I did not think of the Pentateuch as a political document, I did not profile the authorship or the readership of the Pentateuch.

At that time, I saw the Pentateuch as called forth by a theological need—to understand and explain what it was to be the people of God at a threshold moment. Nowadays, I would also try to see the Pentateuch as a political document, the product of some group within Israel designed to influence some other group. I would ask, In whose interests was the Pentateuch written? and What class or sectional programme is being furthered by the Pentateuch? I would not regard the Pentateuch as undifferentiatedly the work of a 'believing community', as the jargon has it, nor as addressing exilic Israel in general. For I now think that Jewish society in the exilic period was the site of serious conflicts, ideological and political, and that it is inconceivable that the Pentateuch would have been equally acceptable to all Jews or would have had the same meaning for all. I would focus on the land as the primary issue here, considering how the Pentateuch's story of movement towards a promised land would serve the interests of that segment of the Babylonian Jews that migrated to the Jewish homeland, and how necessary it was for the Pentateuch to be written for their goals to be achieved. I would try to imagine an alternative Pentateuch, which would have served the interests of Jews who did not belong to the return party. I would be asking, in short, Why is there a Pentateuch?, and answering it not only in literary or theological terms, but also in political terms.

There is another element in a political reading of the Pentateuch. It is the matter of the impact of the Pentateuch upon readers in times later than its own. This was a concern I already had in writing *The Theme of the Pentateuch,* when I dealt in Chapter 10 both with what I called its 'historical' function and its 'theological' function. I meant by 'theological' function the significance its primary theme might have for later readers. But today I would not express the significance of the Pentateuch solely in theological terms, for I would be very mindful, for example, of the strongly political effect of the Pentateuch in modern Israeli debates over the land of Israel. The idea that God has promised a land to a particular nation, that the land lies in such and such a geographical space, and that the land belongs to them in a deeper sense (that is, as a divine gift) than most other nations' lands belong to them—these are ideas of great political importance in our contemporary world. And they are ideas for which the Pentateuch is responsible. In the first edition of *The Theme of the Pentateuch,* the land as such dropped out of sight in the last chapter, and became merely a symbol for a vaguer, more mental and psychological category of 'promise' and 'hope'. I am not repenting of that move I made, but I can see now that the land as a physical entity has more importance that I gave it credit for, and that the Pentateuch is still, what it always was, a political document.

d. The Theology of the Pentateuch

On the whole, *The Theme of the Pentateuch* concerns itself with identifying and describing theological ideas contained in the Pentateuch. It is not much involved in evaluating those ideas. It is true that I said that 'since the Pentateuch is not only a literary work, but also a religious literary work, it would be in bad taste—to say no more—to ignore the contemporary religious function the Pentateuchal theme can have among those who read the Pentateuch as part of their "Scripture"' (p. 17); and the second half of the last chapter was devoted to how the Pentateuch might have a theological meaning to readers of today. What I notice now about that aspect of the book is how the theology of the Pentateuch was evaluated only ever positively. Its 'contemporary religious function' (p. 108) was a good thing, and it could be read off from the two facts that the Pentateuch is a story and that the Pentateuch is built around a promise. The Pentateuch, I argued, creates a 'world', which the reader is invited to enter. It is a world in which life and reality have meaning, and in which living in hope is set forth as an admirable way of being in the world. The implicit message was that the theology of the Pentateuch is good theology, that the Pentateuch is good for us, and that it would be helpful for us to appropriate its message, adapting it and working it out in contemporary religious experience.

In short, what I seemed to be advocating was a rather uncritical acceptance of the ideas of the Pentateuch. I am very interested now to observe that I also said that the Pentateuch's theme might not only 'develop' but also perhaps 'thwart' the reader's consciousness of life and reality (p. 18), and that the reader might not only be 'seized' and 'challenged' by the world that it creates, but also perhaps 'threatened' (p. 126). So I was already allowing that the Pentateuch might not be everyone's cup of tea, that it would be possible, and permissible, to regard the Pentateuch as purveying wrong or unhealthy or one-sided or damaging ideas—and that therefore a critical evaluation, which did not simply swallow its ideas of a chosen people, a promised land, a punishing God and the like, was called for. But I said nothing of what such a critique would look like.

Nowadays I do not want to negate the positive evaluation I made of the theology of the Pentateuch. But I am more inclined to insist, for myself at least, on a critical evaluation of it rather than an unthinking acceptance. I do not need to defend my usual desire to make a critical evaluation of all kinds of things that come my way, but on this matter I do somewhat, out of respect for (shall I say?) the faith of my fathers (and mothers), who could not have allowed the Pentateuch, as part of the Bible, to be criticized in any way. I content myself with only two responses. The first is a prooftext, from Paul; I have long taken comfort in his dictum that 'whatsoever things were written aforetime were written for our learning' (Rom. 15.4 KJV)—which I take to mean, not for our imitation or uncritical adulation or unthinking acceptance, but, for us to use our critical and evaluative judgment upon. The second comes from my experience of writing a commentary on the book of Job,[11] where most of the theology contained in this biblical book is, by the standards even of the book itself, misguided, one-sided or just plain wrong. If the friends are right, Job is wrong, and vice versa; and if God is right, they are all wrong in one way or another; and if the narrator is right and in the end Job's virtue is rewarded, everything that has been said in the book up to that point is either gainsaid or marginalized.[12] Both of these considerations convince me that critical evaluation of a biblical book is not disrespect.

Since *The Theme of the Pentateuch* was written, I have come to feel, not just that critique is possible, and welcome, but that it is requisite, and desirable, if we are to treat the biblical texts with the seriousness they deserve. Nowadays, I am making a fundamental distinction between 'understanding' and 'critique'. This is how I have put it:

> In the project known as 'understanding' (which is the Enlightenment project to which most scholars of the present day still

> subscribe), we aim at a fair-minded, patient and sympathetic re-creation of the meaning, significance and intentions of the ancient text in its own time.[13]

That was essentially the project of *The Theme of the Pentateuch.* But nowadays I want to speak also of the project of critique or evaluation:

> It is a measure of our commitment to our own standards and values that we register disappointment, dismay or disgust when we encounter in the texts of ancient Israel ideologies that we judge to be inferior to ours. And it is a measure of our open-mindedness and eagerness to learn and do better that we remark with pleasure, respect and envy values and ideologies within the biblical texts that we judge to be superior to our own. 'Critique' does not of course imply *negative* evaluation, but it does imply evaluation of the texts by a standard of reference outside themselves—which usually means, for practical purposes, by the standards to which we ourselves are committed ... We have a responsibility, I believe, to evaluate the Bible's claims and assumptions, and if we abdicate that responsibility, whether as scholars or as readers-in-general of the Bible, we are in my opinion guilty of an ethical fault.[14]

What I am now demanding of myself is a more quizzical, more thoughtful, more hesitating reading of the Pentateuch, that calls every assertion it makes into question, not least its assertions about God—not with the aim of rejecting them or belittling them, but in order to know whether, if I adopt them, I do so of my own free will or under the constraint of some external 'authority'.[15]

In practice, that means that I cannot now automatically assume that the theme of the Pentateuch is a wholly desirable position to adopt theologically speaking. Nowadays I have my misgivings, for example, about the claim the Pentateuch makes that one nation was chosen by God, and that that nation was promised by God a land where other people were living. Nowadays I have my misgivings about promises that never seem to be fulfilled, or at least are only ever partially fulfilled. I worry about whether living in hope, despite all the appearances, is as laudable a way of being in the world as I assumed it was when I wrote *The Theme of the Pentateuch*. These days, I am not so sure that the authors of the Pentateuch were speaking on every page in the name of God, and not also (or rather) speaking in the name of the interests, social, political and ideological, that they represented. I have to raise these questions for the sake of a critical reading of the Bible, which my own social and professional location as a university professor rather than, for example, a minister of a church, obliges me to, and which in any case I believe in. So I cannot now urge my readers to adapt themselves to the ideas of the Pentateuch or to let themselves be irresistibly seized by the world that the Pentateuchal story creates. I do not deny its power, and I am happy to admit my own continuing fascination with its challenge to our notions of what it means to be truly human. If I were to write *The Theme of the Pentateuch* again, I should have to explore in depth the critique I have hinted at here. In the meantime, I am delighted if anyone will enter the text of the Pentateuch and experience its intellectual richness and its religious power with the help of this book.

Endnotes

To Chapter One: Method

1 H.W. Wolff, 'The Kerygma of the Yahwist', *Interpretation* 20 (1966), pp. 131-58, originally published in *Evangelische Theologie* 24 (1964), pp. 73-97.

2 H.W. Wolff, 'The Elohistic Fragments in the Pentateuch', *Interpretation* 26 (1972), pp. 158-73, originally published in *Evangelische Theologie* 27 (1969), pp. 59-72.

3 W. Brueggemann, 'The Kerygma of the "Priestly Writers"', *Zeitschrift für die alttestamentliche Wissenschaft* 84 (1972), pp. 397-414.

4 P.F. Ellis, *The Yahwist: The Bible's First Theologian* (London: Chapman, 1969).

5 See T.S. Kuhn, *The Structure of Scientific Revolutions* (International Encyclopedia of Unified Sciences, vol. 2, no. 2; Chicago: Chicago University Press, 2nd edn, 1970), but note his modifications of his thesis and the discussions by J.W.N. Watkins, S.E. Toulmin, L. Pearce Williams and K.R. Popper in particular in I. Lakatos and A. Musgrave (eds.), *Criticism and the Growth of Knowledge* (Proceedings of the International Colloquium in the Philosophy of Science, London, 1965, vol. 4; Cambridge: Cambridge University Press, 1970).

6 Cf. the exposition of the role of the literary critic by Helen Gardner, *The Business of Criticism* (Oxford: Oxford University Press, 1959), pp. 3-24.

7 L. Alonso Schökel describes it thus: 'The *genetic* approach intends to describe the genesis of the work, from its origins, through the stages of tradition, to the end product. Decisive value is attributed to either end of the chain according to the scholar's preferences or convictions. It is a diachronic study, frequently highly hypothetical' (*Narrative Structures in the Book of Judith* [ed. W. Wueller; The Center for Hermeneutical Studies in Hellenistic and Modern Culture. Protocol of the Eleventh Colloquy; Berkeley: The Center for Hermeneutical Studies in Hellenistic and Modern Culture, 1975], p. 19).

8 G. von Rad, *The Problem of the Hexateuch and Other Essays* (trans. E. Trueman Dicken; Edinburgh and London: Oliver & Boyd, 1966), p. 2.

9 M. Noth, *A History of Pentateuchal Traditions* (trans. with an Introduction by Bernhard W. Anderson; Englewood Cliffs, NJ; Prentice–Hall, 1972, originally published, 1948).

10 See, for example, B.S. Childs, 'The Canonical Shape of the Prophetic Literature', *Interpretation* 32 (1978), pp. 46-55; Childs, 'The Exegetical

Significance of Canon for the Study of the Old Testament', in *Congress Volume: Göttingen 1977* (ed. W. Zimmerli *et al.*; Supplements to Vetus Testamentum, 29; Leiden: E.J. Brill, 1978), pp. 66-80.

11 L. Alonso Schökel, 'Hermeneutical Problems of a Literary Study of the Bible', *Supplements to Vetus Testamentum* 28 (1975), pp. 1-15.

12 W. Wink, *The Bible in Human Transformation: Toward a New Paradigm for Biblical Study* (Philadelphia: Fortress, 1973). Cf. also e.g. J.F.A. Sawyer, *From Moses to Patmos: New Perspectives in Old Testament Study* (London: SPCK, 1977), especially pp. 10f.; R. Alter, 'A Literary Approach to the Bible', *Commentary* 60 (1975), pp. 70-77; G.W. Coats, *From Canaan to Egypt: Structural and Theological Context for the Joseph Story* (Catholic Biblical Quarterly Monograph Series, 4; Washington, DC: Catholic Biblical Association of America, 1976), pp. 58ff.; M.A. Fishbane, 'The Sacred Center: The Symbolic Structure of the Bible', in *Texts and Responses* (Festschrift Nahum N. Glatzer; ed. M.A. Fishbane and P.R. Flohr; Leiden: E.J. Brill, 1975), pp. 6-27 (esp. pp. 6f.).

13 G. von Rad, *Genesis: A Commentary* (trans. J.H. Marks; Philadelphia: Westminster, revised edn, 1972), p. 75. Von Rad, however, did not follow his own principle when he came to expound Genesis 6–9, where he dealt with the J and P material separately (pp. 118-30).

14 It is cheering to know that editors of fiction of the nineteenth century (CE) have similar problems to those of biblical critics: on the day the above paragraph was written I read a report of the Thirteenth Annual Conference on Editorial Problems (1977) held in the University of Toronto, at which there were discussed such questions as the distinction between what nineteenth-century novelists actually wrote and what they intended to write (there can be a difference even when the author's manuscript is extant), and the question of what constituted the definitive text of a work from which the author (e.g. Thoreau, Melville) had excised digressions, or that the author (e.g. Hardy) went on improving through several editions. See 'Editorial Responsibilities', *The Times Literary Supplement,* 9 December, 1977, p. 1449.

To Chapter Two: Definitions

1 Noth, *Pentateuchal Traditions.*

2 See Noth, *Pentateuchal Traditions,* pp. 46-62.

3 G. von Rad's statement of 'the basic theme' of the Hexateuch (*Genesis*, pp. 13f.) may be criticized on this ground.

4 'A plot is ... a narrative of events, the emphasis falling on causality. "The king died and then the queen died" is a story. "The king died, and then the queen died of grief" is a plot. The time sequence (sc. of the story) is preserved, but the sense of causality overshadows it' (E.M. Forster,

Aspects of the Novel [Harmondsworth: Penguin, 1962; originally published, 1927], pp. 93f.).

5 Cf. G.W. Coats's understanding of 'theme' as 'structured plot' ('Conquest Traditions in the Wilderness Theme', *Journal of Biblical Literature* 95 [1976], pp. 177-90 [178]).

6 D.L. Petersen, 'A Thrice-Told Tale: Genre, Theme, and Motif', *Biblical Research* 18 (1973), pp. 30-43 (38).

7 W.F. Thrall and A. Hibberd, *A Handbook to Literature* (New York: Odyssey, 1960), p. 486.

8 See in general R.E. Palmer's 'Thirty Theses on Interpretation', in his *Hermeneutics: Interpretation Theory in Schleiermacher, Dilthey, Heidegger, and Gadamer* (Evanston: Northwestern University Press, 1969), pp. 242-53; and in particular Gardner, *Business of Criticism*, p. 15, where she speaks of 'the enlarging and continual reforming of one's conception of a work by bringing fresh knowledge and fresh experience of life and literature to it'.

9 See, e.g., J.D. Crossan (ed.), *Polyvalent Narration, Semeia* 9 (1977).

10 The question of 'intentionality' in the sense of 'author's intention' is too complex to be discussed here, but I have to register my dissatisfaction with the critique by E.D. Hirsch of the view that we do not have access to the author's meaning (*Validity in Interpretation* [New Haven: Yale University Press, 1967], pp. 14-19). The position with (often anonymous) biblical literature is not necessarily the same as with, for example, modern reportage.

11 Defined by J.T. Shipley (ed.), *Dictionary of World Literature* (Totowa, NJ: Littlefield, Adams & Co., 1968), p. 274, as 'a word or pattern of thought that recurs in a similar situation ... to evoke a similar mood, within a work, or in various works of a genre' (cited from Coats, 'Conquest Traditions', p. 178).

12 R. Scholes and R. Kellogg, *The Nature of Narrative* (New York: Oxford University Press, 1966), p. 27, define a *topos* as consisting of a narrative and a conceptual element; so, for example, a combination of a (narrative) motif of a hero's descent to the netherworld and a (conceptual) 'theme' of the search for wisdom.

13 As in W. Arend, *Die typischen Scenen bei Homer* (Berlin: Weidmann, 1933); B. Fenik, *Typical Battle Scenes in the Iliad: Studies in the Narrative Techniques of Homeric Battle Description* (Wiesbaden: Steiner, 1968).

14 As the term has been used by my colleague D.M. Gunn, 'Narrative Patterns and Oral Tradition in Judges and Samuel', *Vetus Testamentum* 24 (1974), pp. 286-317 (see especially 314 n. 2).

15 A.B. Lord defined theme as 'a recurrent element of narration or description in traditional oral poetry' ('Composition by Theme in Homer and Southslavic Epos', *Transactions of the American Philological Association* 82 [1951], pp. 71-80 [73]), and elsewhere as 'groups of ideas regularly used in telling a tale in the formulaic style of traditional song' (the latter

definition cited from Scholes and Kellogg, *Nature of Narrative*, p. 26).
16 For example, the theme of expulsion in Genesis 1–11 (Adam, Cain, the tower-builders), or the theme of the human and the soil (*'ādām* and *'ădāmâ* in the same chapters); see P.D. Miller, Jr, *Genesis 1–11: Studies in Structure and Theme* (Journal for the Study of the Old Testament Supplement Series, 8; Sheffield: JSOT Press, 1978), pp. 37-42.
17 This point seems to be similar to that made in his methodological remarks by M.R. Hauge, 'The Struggles of the Blessed in Estrangement', *Studia Theologica* 29 (1975), pp. 1-30, 113-46 (6 n. 7).
18 R. and M. Thompson, *Critical Reading and Writing* (New York: Random House, 1969), p. 15.
19 A.J. Greimas, *Sémantique structurale: Recherche de méthode* (Paris: Larousse, 1966). For some applications of Greimas's actantial analysis to Old Testament narrative, see R. Barthes, 'The Struggle with the Angel: Textual Analysis of Genesis 32:23-33', in R. Barthes *et al.*, *Structural Analysis and Biblical Exegesis: Interpretational Essays* (Pittsburgh: Pickwick, 1974), pp. 21-33 (30f.); D. Jobling, *The Sense of Biblical Narrative: Three Structural Analyses in the Old Testament* (Journal for the Study of the Old Testament Supplement Series, 7; Sheffield: JSOT Press, 1978). See also on the subject R.M. Polzin, *Biblical Structuralism: Method and Subjectivity in the Study of Ancient Texts* (Philadelphia: Fortress, and Missoula: Scholars Press, 1977), esp. pp. 54-125.
20 Cf. the definition of theme by Thrall and Hibberd quoted above: 'the central or dominating idea in a literary work ... the abstract concept which is made concrete' (note 7 above).
21 Von Rad, *Problem of the Hexateuch*, p. 2.
22 Noth, *Pentateuchal Traditions*, p. 250.
23 Noth, *Pentateuchal Traditions*, p. 251.
24 Von Rad, *Genesis*, p. 13.
25 Noth, *Pentateuchal Traditions*, p. 250.

To Chapter Three: Indicators

1 B.S. Childs, *Exodus* (London: SCM Press, 1974), p. 638.
2 The other place names in the verse have proved unidentifiable; see the commentaries.
3 W. Zimmerli, *Man and His Hope in the Old Testament* (Studies in Biblical Theology, II/20; London: SCM Press, 1971; originally published 1968), p. 50.
4 See conveniently for a brief statement and bibliography, C. Westermann, 'Promises to the Patriarchs', in *Interpreter's Dictionary of the Bible. Supplementary Volume* (ed. K. Crim; Nashville: Abingdon, 1976), pp. 690-93.
5 Cf. C. Westermann, *Die Verheissungen an die Väter: Studien zur Vätergeschichte* (Forschungen zur Religion und Literatur des Alten und

Neuen Testaments, 116; Göttingen: Vandenhoeck & Ruprecht, 1976), esp. pp. 123-49.

6 See Westermann, 'Promises', p. 691a.

To Chapter Five: Formulations

1 R. Rendtorff, *Das überlieferungsgeschichtliche Problem des Pentateuchs* (Beihefte zur *Zeitschrift für die alttestamentliche Wissenschaft*, 147; Berlin: de Gruyter, 1977), p. 48 (ET *The Problem of the Process of Transmission in the Pentateuch* [trans. J.J. Scullion; Journal for the Study of the Old Testament Supplement Series, 89; Sheffield: JSOT Press, 1990], pp. 64-65).

2 C. Westermann, 'Arten der Erzählung in der Genesis', in his *Forschung am Alten Testament* (Munich: Chr. Kaiser, 1964), pp. 9-91 (25f.).

3 As does Rendtorff, *Problem*, p. 49.

4 So LXX.

To Chapter Six: Exposition

1 'The most frequent promise in Gen. 12–50 is that of posterity, with that of the land a distant second' (Westermann, 'Promises', p. 691).

2 He also is heir to the promise of descendants (16.10; 21.13, 18), though not apparently to the other elements of the promise.

3 See especially the elaborate, though sometimes obscure, exploration of this pattern by Hauge, 'The Struggles of the Blessed in Estrangement', *Studia Theologica* 29 (1975), pp. 1-30, 113-46.

4 See e.g. Wolff, 'The Kerygma of the Yahwist', p. 139.

5 The reason Moses gives 'does ring a bit hollow', comments Childs (*Exodus*, p. 160), but only within the context of the narrative unit—not within the context of the theme of the Pentateuch as a whole.

6 Once again I think that Childs's comment that 'all [the themes of this chapter] circle about the role of the faithful mediator, Moses, who wrestles with God for the sake of Israel' (*Exodus*, p. 599) is true only within the context of the chapter or perhaps of the entire Moses narrative, but not within the context of the Pentateuch as a whole.

7 Childs, *Exodus*, p. 595.

8 J.R. Porter, *Leviticus* (Cambridge Bible Commentary; Cambridge: Cambridge University Press, 1976), p. 7.

9 See G.I. Davies, 'The Wilderness Itineraries: A Comparative Study', *Tyndale Bulletin* 25 (1974), pp. 46-81 (80).

10 J. de Vaulx, *Les Nombres* (Sources bibliques; Paris: Gabalda, 1972), p. 12.

11 J. Sturdy, *Numbers* (Cambridge Bible Commentary; Cambridge: Cambridge University Press, 1976), p. 74.

12 On these chapters, see now Jobling, *The Sense of Biblical Narrative: Three Structural Analyses in the Old Testament.*
13 Cf. G.B. Gray, *A Critical and Exegetical Commentary on Numbers* (International Critical Commentary; Edinburgh: T. & T. Clark, 1912), p. 151; for a contrary interpretation, see M.S. Seale, 'Numbers xiii.32', *Expository Times* 68 (1956–57), p. 28.
14 If that phrase is to be so understood (cf. Sturdy, *Numbers*, pp. 116f.). Strangely, but perhaps not so strangely, it is the fate of those who refuse to 'go up' (*'lh*) into the land (16.12, 14) that they 'go down' (*yrd*) alive into the ground/land to Sheol (16.31ff.).
15 S.R. Driver, *A Critical and Exegetical Commentary on Deuteronomy* (International Critical Commentary; Edinburgh: T. & T. Clark, 3rd edn, 1902), pp. lxxix-lxxx.
16 For the statistics in this paragraph, see Driver, *Deuteronomy*, pp. lxxviii-lxxxi.

To Chapter Seven: Prefatory Theme

1 Von Rad, *Genesis*, pp. 152f.
2 Westermann, 'Arten der Erzählung', p. 47.
3 Von Rad, *Genesis*, p. 153.
4 Westermann, 'Arten der Erzählung', p. 56, sees a mitigation in the fact that the punishment is *only* a shortening of life; but this view is unlikely since no hint is given in the narrative that the punishment could have been more severe. If the sons of God episode is closely connected with the Flood narrative, the element of mitigation can be seen in the deliverance of Noah.
5 On the question whether Noah is regarded as typical of his generation or as 'righteous' only in view of God's deliverance of him, see W.M. Clark, 'The Righteousness of Noah', *Vetus Testamentum* 21 (1971), pp. 261-80; A.N. Barnard, 'Was Noah a Righteous Man?', *Theology* 84 (1971), pp. 311-14.
6 Von Rad, *Genesis*, p. 75.
7 Von Rad, *Genesis*, pp. 152f.; cf. also his *Theology of the Old Testament* (trans. D.M.G. Stalker; Edinburgh: Oliver & Boyd, 1962), I, pp. 154ff. Similarly already H. Gunkel, *Genesis* (Göttingen: Vandenhoeck & Ruprecht, 6th edn, 1964), p. 1, noting themes of human sin, God's wrath and God's grace; and J. Skinner, A *Critical and Exegetical Commentary on Genesis* (International Critical Commentary; Edinburgh: T. & T. Clark, 2nd edn, 1930), p. 2, who thought that the units of the primaeval history were arranged 'with perhaps a certain unity of conception, in so far as they illustrate the increasing wickedness that accompanied the progress of mankind in civilisation'.

8 D. Kidner, *Genesis* (Tyndale Old Testament Commentaries; London: Tyndale Press, 1967), p. 13.

9 Cf. e.g. M.D. Johnson, *The Purpose of the Biblical Genealogies with Special Reference to the Setting of the Genealogies of Jesus* (Society for New Testament Studies Monograph Series, 8; Cambridge: Cambridge University Press, 1969), pp. 14, 26ff., who distinguishes between the genealogies of J and P, finding in the genealogies of J no particular purpose beyond showing the 'interrelation of a certain number of tribes', but in P certain theological purposes, notably to set the stage for the emergence of the chosen people and to trace the narrowing of the line down to Aaron. For a more positive evaluation of the theological significance of the Genesis genealogies, see R.R. Wilson, *Genealogy and History in the Biblical World* (New Haven: Yale University Press, 1977), esp. pp. 154f., 163-66.

10 On the precise significance of the phrase, see I.M. Kikawada, 'Two Notes on Eve', *Journal of Biblical Literature* 91 (1972), pp. 33-37.

11 So C. Westermann, *Genesis* (Biblischer Kommentar: Altes Testament 1/1; Neukirchen: Neukirchener Verlag, 1966), p. 24.

12 Even in the eschatological age pictured in Isa. 65.20, 100 years is the normal span of life.

13 The two exceptions are Enoch (365 years) and Lamech (777 years). It seems undeniable that both these figures have a symbolic significance: the 365 years of Enoch correspond to the number of the days of the solar year, Enoch's counterpart (the seventh) in the Sumerian King List being Enmeduranki, king of Sippar, the centre of sun-worship (cf., e.g., E.A. Speiser, *Genesis* [Anchor Bible; New York: Doubleday, 1964], p. 43). Lamech's 777 years are presumably to be related to the 'sword-song' of the Lamech of Gen. 4.24: 'If Cain is avenged sevenfold, truly Lamech seventy-sevenfold'.

14 The progressive decline, both for antediluvians and postdiluvians, is most consistent in the Samaritan version, but the text-critical value of this version at this point is dubious. A similar progressive decline is apparently exhibited in a portion of the Sumerian King List relating to the first six kings of Kish (they reign 1200, 900 [variant 960], 670, 420, 300, 240 years respectively), though the parallel with Genesis 5 has been held to be merely fortuitous (T.C. Hartman, 'Some Thoughts on the Sumerian King List and Genesis 5 and 11B', *Journal of Biblical Literature* 91 [1972], pp. 25-32 [30 n. 19]). We might compare also Hesiod's picture of history as a declining succession of metals (*Works and Days* 1.148) as further evidence of an ancient conception of history as a decline.

15 Von Rad, *Genesis*, pp. 69f., quoting F. Delitzsch. A connection with the 'tree of life' of ch. 3 as the explanation of the longevity of the patriarchs is however too fanciful.

16 The fact that the two genealogies derive from different sources, according to the usual analysis, is not relevant to our present concern with the final form of the text.

17 We may perhaps compare with the Cainite genealogy the list of the Seven Sages of antediluvian times who appear in Mesopotamian texts to be the founders of the arts of civilization; cf. J.J. Finkelstein, 'The Antediluvian Kings: A University of California Tablet', *Journal of Cuneiform Studies* 17 (1963), pp. 39-51 (50 n. 41); and E. Reiner, 'The Etiological Myth of the Seven Sages', *Orientalia* 30 (1961), pp. 1-11.

18 Cf. T.E. Fretheim, *Creation, Fall and Flood: Studies in Genesis 1–11* (Minneapolis: Augsburg, 1969), p. 101; and J.L. McKenzie, 'Reflections on Wisdom', *Journal of Biblical Literature* 86 (1967), pp. 1-9 (6): 'The culture myths have been woven into a sequence of events in which the progress of culture marches with the growth of human pride and wickedness'.

19 I leave aside the criticism of I. Soisalon-Soininen ('Die Urgeschichte im Geschichtswerk des Jahwisten', *Temenos* 6 [1970], pp. 130-41), that there is no need to attribute any theological plan to the Yahwistic primaeval history and that the Yahwist's traditional material effectively determined its own position in his narrative (brother-murder must follow creation of primaeval pair; flood that almost annihilates humankind must follow genealogy of humankind's multiplication and story of its motivation, the angel-marriages and so on). On one level that may be so; but we are here considering whether the work (whether of the Yahwist or of the final redactor) has any conceptual theme beyond a merely 'logical' development.

20 So R. Rendtorff, 'Genesis 8_{21} und die Urgeschichte des Jahwisten', *Kerygma und Dogma* 7 (1961), pp. 69-78 (75); W.M. Clark, 'The Flood and the Structure of the Pre-patriarchal History', *Zeitschrift für die alttestamentliche Wissenschaft* 83 (1971), pp. 184-211 (206); Fretheim, *Creation, Fall and Flood*, p. 20.

21 That is, that the 'sons of God' are dynastic rulers; cf. M.G. Kline, 'Divine Kingship and Genesis 6:1-4', *Westminster Theological Journal* 24 (1962), pp. 187-204; F. Dexinger, *Sturz der Gottersöhne oder Engel vor der Sintflut?* (Vienna: Herder, 1966). I would want to add that they are *also* (semi-) divine beings, like Gilgamesh, two-thirds god and one-third human (*Gilgamesh* 1.2.1; J.B. Pritchard [ed.], *Ancient Near Eastern Texts Relating to the Old Testament* [Princeton: Princeton University Press, 2nd edn, 1955], p. 73b).

22 'Man's attempt to overstep the bounds of creatureliness' (Fretheim, *Creation, Fall and Flood*, p. 123). On the theme of *hybris*, see P. Humbert, 'Démesure et chute dans l'A.T.', in *maqqél shâqédh. La Branche d'amandier: Hommage à Wilhelm Vischer* (ed. S. Amsler *et al.*; Montpellier: Causse, Graille, Castelnau, 1960), pp. 63-82. On the sin of Babel as the attempt to acquire a 'name', viz. a reaching for self-glorification, see A. de Pury, 'La Tour de Babel et la vocation d'Abraham: Notes exégétiques', *Etudes théologiques et religieuses* 53 (1978), pp. 80-97 (89f.).

23 See note 20 above.

24 Rendtorff, 'Genesis 8_{21}', p. 74.

25 Clark, 'Flood and Structure', p. 207.
26 Fretheim, *Creation, Fall and Flood*, p. 113.
27 For two independent examinations of Rendtorff's view, reaching similar conclusions, see O.H. Steck, 'Genesis 12:1-3 und die Urgeschichte des Jahwisten', in *Probleme biblischer Theologie. Gerhard von Rad zum 70. Geburtstag* (ed. H.W. Wolff; Munich: Chr. Kaiser, 1971), pp. 525-54 (527-42); D.L. Petersen, 'The Yahwist on the Flood', *Vetus Testamentum* 26 (1976), pp. 438-46 (442f.).
28 Rendtorff, 'Genesis 8_{21}', p. 70.
29 *lō'-'ōsif lĕqallēl 'ôd 'et-hā'ădāmâ* 'I shall not again curse the ground', parallel to *lō'-'ōsif 'ôd lĕhakkôt 'et-kol-ḥay* 'I shall not again smite everything living'.
30 For a parallel, cf. 3.16 'your desire [the rare word *tĕšûqâ*] shall be toward your husband, but he will rule (*māšal*) over you', with 4.7 '[sin's] desire (*tĕšûqâ*) is toward you, but you will rule (*māšal*) over it'. There is no connection of substance between the content of these passages. For another parallel, see n. 32 below.
31 Clark, 'Flood and Structure', p. 208; cf. Rendtorff, 'Genesis 8_{21}', p. 74.
32 H. Holzinger, *Genesis* (Kurzer Hand-Commentar zum Alten Testament; Freiburg: J.C.B. Mohr, 1898), pp. 60f.; Gunkel, *Genesis*, p. 55; Skinner, *Genesis*, pp. 133f. The observation made by U. Cassuto, *Commentary on Genesis* (Jerusalem; Magnes Press, 1961), I, p. 303, that the roots of 'relief', 'work', and 'toil' (*nḥm, 'śh, 'ṣb*) in 5.29 occur in the same sequence in 6.6, does not destroy the connection of substance between 5.29 and 9.20. 6.6 provides another example of verbal mimicry to add to those mentioned above (n. 30).
33 It may also be objected that the strongly marked element of mitigation in Genesis 3–8 makes it inappropriate to label this an age of the curse.
34 W. Brueggemann, 'David and His Theologian', *Catholic Biblical Quarterly* 30 (1968), pp. 156-81.
35 Brueggemann, 'David and His Theologian', p. 158.
36 For another critique, see Clark, 'Flood and Structure', pp. 201f.
37 Being confined to motifs of wickedness that is punished, but from which Yahweh delivers Noah/David and makes a new beginning.
38 Brueggemann, 'David and His Theologian', p. 167 and n. 45.
39 T. Klaehn, *Die sprachliche Verwandschaft der Quelle K (2 Sam 9ff) der Samuelbücher mit J des Heptateuchs* (Borna-Leipzig: Noske, 1914); J. Blenkinsopp, 'Theme and Motif in the Succession History (2 Sam xi 2ff) and the Yahwist Corpus', *Vetus Testamentum* 15 (1966), pp. 44-57.
40 From another point of view, a relationship between the primaeval history and Jerusalem court traditions in general (not specifically David material) has been claimed by W. Richter, 'Urgeschichte und Hoftheologie', *Biblische Zeitschrift* 10 (1966), pp. 96-105.
41 Even if the Davidic narrative is historically reliable—a view that

seems much less certain now than in 1968 when Brueggemann's article was published (cf. e.g. the role of traditional story-telling elements within it; see D.M. Gunn, 'Traditional Composition in the "Succession Narrative"', *Vetus Testamentum* 26 [1976], pp. 214-29)—the conception of the work and the choice of material from the doubtless greater bulk of Davidic material available could well follow a traditional or developmental sequence such as it displayed in the primaeval history. Brueggemann's case depends on the assumptions that the David story is '(a) historically reliable, and (b) chronologically prior to the other piece' ('David and His Theologian', p. 158 n. 17).

42 See also D.J.A. Clines, 'The Theology of the Flood Narrative', *Faith and Thought* 100 (1972–73), pp. 128-42.

43 J. Blenkinsopp, in J. Blenkinsopp *et al.*, *The Pentateuch* (Chicago; ACTA, 1971), pp. 46f.

44 See Clines, 'Flood Narrative', pp. 138f.

45 Traditional source analysis, assigning 8.3, 7, 13a, 22 and parts of ch. 10 to J and 8.13b, 17; 9.1-17 and parts of ch. 10 to P, fails to observe how deeply imprinted this element is upon the whole text in its final form.

46 Von Rad, *Genesis*, p. 94.

47 Does not our text of Gen. 4.1f., in which one conception but two births are spoken of, already imply this interpretation, common in rabbinic exegesis? Cf. Ps.-Jonathan *in loc.*; Ber. R. xxii 2; TB *Sanh.* 38b. Even Skinner, *Genesis*, p. 103, acknowledges that this 'may very well be the meaning'.

48 It is no disproof of this belief that the Cain and Abel story belongs to the well-known folktale type of 'the hostile brothers' (cf. Westermann, *Genesis*, pp. 428ff.). Such stories are popular just because they are contrary to expectation, like tales of 'the unlikely hero'.

49 So F.W. Bassett, 'Noah's Nakedness and the Curse of Canaan', *Vetus Testamentum* 21 (1971), pp. 232-37; though cf. also G. Rice, 'The Curse that Never Was', *Journal of Religious Thought* 29 (1972), pp. 5-27 (11ff.) for criticism of this view.

50 Cf. similarly Brueggemann, 'David and His Theologian', pp. 175f.

51 Von Rad, *Genesis*, p. 153.

52 Hence, I suppose, von Rad's indecisiveness on this question. On p. 152 of his *Genesis* we find that the Babel story is the end of the primaeval history, and on p. 154 that the 'real conclusion' is 12.1-3, while on pp. 161ff. 12.4-9 is included in the primaeval history.

53 See above, a. 2. b. (1) in the present chapter.

54 It limits our horizons unnecessarily to read Gen. 12.1-3 solely within the context of the Yahwist's work, as de Pury does in his otherwise perceptive study, 'La Tour de Babel', pp. 92f.

55 See B. Albrektson, *History and the Gods: An Essay on the Idea of Historical Events as Divine Manifestations in the Ancient Near East and in Israel* (Lund: Gleerup, 1967), pp. 78-81.

To Chapter Eight: Divergences

1 Von Rad, *Theology of the Old Testament*, I, pp. 129-35.
2 Von Rad, *Theology of the Old Testament*, I, p. 133.
3 Von Rad, *Theology of the Old Testament*, I, p. 134.
4 Von Rad, *Theology of the Old Testament*, I, p. 134.
5 Von Rad, *Theology of the Old Testament*, I, p. 134.
6 Von Rad, *Theology of the Old Testament*, I, p. 135.
7 Perhaps in the background to von Rad's covenantal structure lies J. Wellhausen's description of P as the Book of the Four Covenants (*Die Composition des Hexateuchs* [Berlin: Reimer, 1899], pp. 1f.).
8 Von Rad, *Theology of the Old Testament*, I, p. 129.
9 Von Rad, *Theology of the Old Testament*, I, p. 133.
10 Von Rad, *Theology of the Old Testament*, I, p. 134.
11 Von Rad, *Theology of the Old Testament*, I, p. 303.
12 Von Rad, *Theology of the Old Testament*, I, p. 304.
13 B.T. Dahlberg, 'On Recognizing the Unity of Genesis', *Theology Digest* 24 (1977), pp. 360-67.
14 Dahlberg, 'Unity of Genesis', p. 361.
15 Dahlberg, 'Unity of Genesis', p. 364.
16 Dahlberg, 'Unity of Genesis', p. 365. The blessings to Laban (30.27, 30) and to Esau (33.10) should perhaps also be mentioned.
17 So, for example, Coats, *From Canaan to Egypt*.
18 Dahlberg, 'Unity of Genesis', p. 366.
19 Dahlberg, 'Unity of Genesis', p. 366.
20 B.A. Levine, 'Numbers, Book of', in *Interpreter's Dictionary of the Bible. Supplementary Volume* (ed. K. Crim; Nashville: Abingdon, 1976), pp. 631-35 (634).
21 N.H. Snaith, *Leviticus. Numbers* (New Century Bible; London: Nelson, 1967), pp. 4f.
22 Gray, *Numbers*, pp. xxiii-xxiv.
23 Gray, *Numbers*, pp. xxiv-xxv.
24 H. Holzinger, *Numeri* (Kurzer Hand-Commentar zum Alten Testament: Tübingen: J.C.B. Mohr, 1903), p. x.
25 A.R.S. Kennedy, *Leviticus and Numbers* (Century Bible; Edinburgh: T.C. & E.C. Jack, 1901), p. 185.
26 For a more positive evaluation of Numbers, see O. Eissfeldt, *The Old Testament: An Introduction* (trans. P.R. Ackroyd; Oxford: Blackwell, 1966), pp. 156f.; and for a brief attempt to account for the content and sequence of Numbers 5–6, see U. Cassuto, 'The Sequence and Arrangement of the Biblical Sections' [1947], in *Biblical and Oriental Studies* (Jerusalem: Magnes Press, 1973), I, pp. 1-6 (3f.).

Endnotes

To Chapter Nine: Literary History

1 See Rendtorff, *Problem;* H.H. Schmid, *Der sogennante Jahwist* (Zurich: Theologischer Verlag, 1976); J. Van Seters, *Abraham in History and Tradition* (New Haven: Yale University Press, 1975). For discussion of the issues, see *Journal for the Study of the Old Testament* 3 (1977), pp. 2-60.

2 G. Fohrer, *Introduction to the Old Testament* (trans. D. Green; London: SPCK, 1970), p. 194.

3 O. Kaiser, *Introduction to the Old Testament* (trans. J. Sturdy; Oxford: Blackwell, 1975), p. 79.

4 Eissfeldt, *Introduction*, p. 200.

5 A. Weiser, *Introduction to the Old Testament* (trans. D.M. Barton; London: Darton, Longman & Todd, 1961), p. 101.

6 Noth, *History of Pentateuchal Traditions*, pp. 55f.

7 Von Rad, *Old Testament Theology*, I, p. 134.

8 Von Rad, *Old Testament Theology*, I, p. 133.

9 Wolff, 'Kerygma of the Yahwist'.

10 J. Hoftijzer, *Die Verheissungen an die drei Erzväter* (Leiden: E.J. Brill, 1956).

11 Westermann, *Verheissungen an die Väter.*

12 R.E. Clements, *Abraham and David: Genesis XV and Its Meaning for Israelite Tradition* (Studies in Biblical Theology, II/5; London: SCM Press, 1967), p. 15.

13 See the Introductions.

14 G. von Rad, 'Ancient Word and Living Word: The Preaching of Deuteronomy and Our Preaching', *Interpretation* 15 (1961), pp. 3-13 (4).

15 Fohrer, *Introduction*, p. 177.

16 Kaiser, *Introduction*, p. 105.

17 Brueggemann, 'Kerygma of the "Priestly Writers"', p. 400.

18 Brueggemann, 'Kerygma of the "Priestly Writers"', pp. 400f.

19 J. Blenkinsopp, 'The Structure of P', *Catholic Biblical Quarterly* 38 (1976), pp. 275-92.

20 Cf. Blenkinsopp, 'The Structure of P', p. 289.

21 I leave E aside as too fragmentary a work for its theme to be established, though one may certainly speak of dominant motifs in it (cf. e.g. Wolff, 'The Elohistic Fragments in the Pentateuch').

22 See notes 2 and 3 above, and also von Rad, *The Problem of the Hexateuch*, p. 73; Beatrice L. Goff, 'The Lost Yahwistic Account of the Conquest of Canaan', *Journal of Biblical Literature* 53 (1934), pp. 241-49.

23 Wolff, 'Kerygma of the Yahwist', p. 140.

24 My italics.

25 Wolff, 'Kerygma of the Yahwist', pp. 154f.

26 Zimmerli, *Man and His Hope*, p. 55.

27 Von Rad, 'Ancient Word and Living Word', p. 7.

28 Cf. J. Moltmann, *Theology of Hope: On the Ground and Implications of a Christian Eschatology* (trans. J.W. Leitch; London: SCM Press, 1967), pp. 103f.
29 K. Elliger, 'Sinn und Ursprung der priesterschriftlichen Geschichtserzählung', *Zeitschrift für Theologie und Kirche* 49 (1952), pp. 121-43; Noth, *History of Pentateuchal Traditions,* p. 10; Brueggemann, 'Kerygma of "Priestly Writers"', p. 399.
30 Brueggemann, 'Kerygma of "Priestly Writers"', p. 413.
31 Zimmerli, *Man and His Hope,* p. 68.

To Chapter Ten: Function

1 Not necessarily its final form as preserved in the Massoretic text; orthographic changes, glosses, and minor additions may have occurred to the 'final shape' without affecting its general significance.
2 So e.g. J. Wellhausen, *Prolegomena to the History of Ancient Israel* (New York: Meridian, r.p. 1957), p. 408; Fohrer, *Introduction,* p. 192; Eissfeldt, *Introduction*, p. 238.
3 Kaiser, *Introduction*, p. 108.
4 Cf. Neh. 10.31 with Exod. 34.16 (J); Neh. 10.32 with Deut. 15.2 (D); Neh. 8.13ff. with Lev. 23.40.
5 Von Rad, 'Ancient Word and Living Word', p. 8.
6 Cf. K. Koch, 'Ezra and the Origins of Judaism', *Journal of Semitic Studies* 19 (1974), pp. 173-97 (184-89).
7 For some instructive examples of the kinds of abuse the Old Testament can suffer when attempts are made to press it into the service of various contemporary presuppositions, see G.G. Harrop, *Elijah Speaks Today: The Long Road into Naboth's Vineyard* (Nashville: Abingdon, 1975).
8 Cf. J. Barr, 'Story and History in Biblical Theology', *Journal of Religion* 16 (1976), pp. 1-17. See further also D. Ritschl and H.O. Jones, *'Story' als Rohmaterial der Theologie* (Theologische Existenz heute, Nr. 192; Munich: Chr. Kaiser, 1976); Jones's contribution appears in somewhat shortened form in his article, 'The Concept of Story and Theological Discourse', *Scottish Journal of Theology* 29 (1976), pp. 415-33.
9 See here J.A. Wharton, 'The Occasion of the Word of God: An Unguarded Essay on the Character of the Old Testament as the Memory of God's Story with Israel', *Austin Seminary Bulletin: Faculty Edition* 84 (Sept. 1968), pp. 3-54, esp. pp. 18, 21-31, for some provocative thoughts about the potential applicability of the label 'story' to the Old Testament literature.
10 The best bibliography on 'story' known to me is that presented by John Navone, *Towards a Theology of Story* (Slough: St Paul Publications, 1977), pp. 153-56. The analysis of story by J.D. Crossan, *The Dark Interval* (Niles, IL: Argus, 1975), esp. pp. 57-62, into the categories of myth, apologue,

action, satire, and parable, is valuable. But Crossan's work is an apologia for parable as 'world-subverting', while myth (which is how I suppose he would categorize the Pentateuch) is 'world-establishing', and therefore at the opposite end of the spectrum from parable. I do not, however, believe with Crossan that the essence of these types of story can be expressed simply as 'comfort' (myth) and 'challenge' (parable), since the 'world' of any story—myth or parable—can act as either, depending on the reader's stance.

11 In one of his finest paragraphs, Kornelis H. Miskotte writes: 'In our conviction the Bible is essentially a narrative, a story, which we must pass on by retelling it. And in this way it can come about that the story may 'happen'—so to speak, in an 'unbloody repetition'—to those who listen to us. Look!—this is the way God dealt with men back there; but because it is he, will he not also deal with you in the same way? Yes, as soon as you discover who this He is, your telling of the story will begin to run; if you are united with that other life outside and beyond your own, then your own drama of salvation will begin to unfold and show that it is already moving toward its solution—how, you yourself do not know' (*When the Gods are Silent* [trans. John W. Doberstein; London: Collins, 1967], p. 204).

12 On the concept of the 'merging of horizons' (*Horizontverschmelzung*), see H.G. Gadamer, *Truth and Method* (New York: Seabury, 1975), pp. 269-73. I have previously employed this conception in my interpretation of Isaiah 53: *I, He, We, and They: A Literary Approach to Isaiah 53* (Journal for the Study of the Old Testament Supplement Series, 1; Sheffield: JSOT Press, 1976), pp. 54ff. For an analysis of the functioning of story, see further W. Wink, 'On Wrestling with God: Using Psychological Insights in Biblical Study', *Religion in Life* 47 (1978), pp. 136-47. He quotes a report of an American Plains Indian's view of story which is apposite here: 'Whenever we hear a Story, it is as if we were physically walking down a particular path that has been created for us. Everything we perceive upon this path or around it becomes part of our experience, both individually and collectively' (p. 143; cited from H. Storm, *Seven Arrows* [New York: Ballantine, 1973], p. 17).

13 Robert P. Roth, *Story and Reality: An Essay on Truth* (Grand Rapids: Eerdmans, 1973), esp. ch. 3 'The Nature of Story' (pp. 20-32).

14 See D.J.A. Clines, 'Predestination in the Old Testament', in *Grace Unlimited* (ed. C.H. Pinnock; Minneapolis: Bethany, 1975), pp. 110-26.

15 Cf. Wharton's pointed question, 'Did they [successive communities of Judaism] remember "rightly" or "wrongly"? ... The first fact is that they did so remember and that the character of that memory shaped the communities of faith which followed' (p. 24).

16 Roth, *Story and Reality*, p. 22.

17 One is reminded of Kierkegaard's slightly different metaphor in his brilliant homily, 'How to Derive True Benediction from Beholding Oneself

in the Mirror of the Word', in *For Self-Examination. Proposed to this Age* (1851), in S. Kierkegaard, *For Self-Examination and Judge for Yourselves! and Three Discourses* (trans. W. Lowrie; London: Oxford University Press, 1946), esp. pp. 50-60.

18 Aristotle, *Poetics*, chs. 7, 23 (= *Classical Literary Criticism. Aristotle: On the Art of Poetry. Horace: On the Art of Poetry. Longinus: On the Sublime* [translated with an introduction by T.S. Dorch; Harmondsworth: Penguin, 1965], pp. 41, 65).

19 For a brief analysis and an example of a movement against the stream, see B. Towers, *Teilhard de Chardin* (London: Lutterworth, 1966), esp. p. 30.

20 Cf. M. Buber, *Moses: The Revelation and the Covenant* (Oxford: East and West Library, 1946): 'The early narrator of the deeds of Moses aimed not at beautiful or instructive sagas, but at a continuity of events ... The connection of episodes derives ... from a powerful primitive emotion which is the passionate recollection of a sequence of unheard-of events' (pp. 17f.).

21 Perhaps the Massoretic vocalization of the first word as *bĕrē'šît* 'in beginning (?)', rather than *bārē'šît* 'in *the* beginning', already reveals an early awareness of the absoluteness of the Pentateuch's beginning.

22 G. Marcel, *Homo Viator: Introduction to a Metaphysic of Hope* (London: Gollancz, 1951). Marcel writes: 'Perhaps a stable order can only be established on earth if man always remains acutely conscious that his condition is that of a traveller' (pp. 7, 153).

23 P. Zweig, *The Adventurer* (London: Dent, 1974), pp. 6f.

24 Navone, *Theology of Story*, p. 53.

25 The sense of being lost or rootless, 'pervasive in contemporary culture', has been analysed in a brilliant fashion by W. Brueggemann (*The Land: Place as Gift, Promise, and Challenge in Biblical Faith* [Philadelphia: Fortress, 1977]), esp. pp. 1-6. However, his emphasis on *land* as a 'central, if not the central theme of biblical faith' seems to me to underplay both the positive cultural and psychological roles of 'cutting loose' and thus being uprooted and also the positive biblical evaluation of strangerhood, exile, and being on the move.

26 *Odyssey* 1.3-5.

27 *Aeneid* 1.3-5. The translation is Dryden's.

28 J. Moltmann, *Theology of Hope: On the Ground and Implications of a Christian Eschatology* (trans. J.W. Leitch; London: SCM Press, 1967), pp. 103-106.

29 W. Zimmerli, 'Promise and Fulfilment', in *Essays on Old Testament Interpretation* (ed. C. Westermann; London: SCM Press, 1963), pp. 89-122. Zimmerli's article first appeared as 'Verheissung und Erfüllung', in *Evangelische Theologie* 12 (1952).

30 Moltmann, *Theology of Hope*, p. 103.

31 Cf. J.B. Cobb, Jr, 'What is the Future? A Process Perspective', in *Hope and the Future of Man* (ed. Ewart H. Cousins; London: The Teilhard Centre for the Future of Man, 1972), pp. 1-14 (1f.).
32 Theognis, *Elegies* 1.637f.
33 Sophocles, *Antigone*, 615f.
34 See R. Bultmann, '*Elpis, elpizo, ap-, proelpizo*', in *Theological Dictionary of the New Testament* (ed. G. Kittel and G. Friedrich), II, pp. 517-21.
35 B. Pascal, *Pensées*, no. 84 (trans. J. Warrington; London: Dent, 1960), pp. 28f.
36 Pope, *Essay on Man*, Epistle 1, line 95.
37 Quoted from Moltmann, *Theology of Hope*, p. 27.
38 E. Bloch, *Das Prinzip Hoffnung* (Berlin: Aufbau-Verlag, 1954–59).
39 W. Pannenberg, 'The God of Hope', in *Basic Questions in Theology* (London: SCM Press, 1971), II, pp. 234-49 (238) (ET of 'Der Gott der Hoffnung', in *Ernst Bloch zu ehren* [ed. S. Unseld; Frankfurt: Suhrkamp, 1965], pp. 209-25 [213]).
40 J. Moltmann, 'Die Kategorie *Novum* in der christlichen Theologie', in *Ernst Bloch zu ehren* [ed. S. Unseld; Frankfurt: Suhrkamp, 1965], pp. 243-63 (243).
41 E. Bloch, *Man on His Own: Essays in the Philosophy of Religion* (New York: Herder & Herder, 1970), p. 69.
42 Zimmerli, *Man and His Hope*, p. 161.
43 Moltmann, *Theology of Hope*, p. 103.
44 J.M. Gustafson, 'The Conditions of Hope: Reflections on Human Experience', *Continuum* 7 (1970), pp. 535-45 (536).
45 Quoted by J.B. Metz, 'Creative Hope', *Cross Currents* 17 (1967), pp. 171-79 (171); reprinted in *New Theology* 5 (ed. M.E. Marty and D.G. Peerman; London: Macmillan, 1968), pp. 130-41 (131).
46 W.W. Meissner, SJ, 'Notes on the Psychology of Hope', *Journal of Religion and Health* 12 (1973), pp. 7-29, 120-39 (17).
47 See E. Stotland, *The Psychology of Hope* (San Francisco: Jossey–Bass, 1969); S. Louthan, 'The Practice of Hope', *Journal of Psychology and Theology* 2 (1974), pp. 276-83; I.M. Korner, 'Hope as a Method of Coping', *Journal of Consultative and Clinical Psychology* 34 (1970), pp. 134-39.
48 Meissner, 'Notes on the Psychology of Hope', pp. 20f.
49 Moltmann, *Theology of Hope*, p. 103.
50 Moltmann, *Theology of Hope*, p. 103 (italics mine).
51 Zimmerli, 'Promise and Fulfilment', p. 97.
52 Metz, 'Creative Hope', p. 171 (= *New Theology* 5, p. 131). Elsewhere Metz argues that the memory of *suffering* is creative for the future in that such memory is subversive of the present ('The Future *Ex Memoria Passionis*', in *Hope and the Future of Man* (ed. Ewart H. Cousins; London: The Teilhard Centre for the Future of Man, 1972), pp. 116-31 (125f.). But this selectivity I find rather one-sided.

53 Cf. the comments to this effect by e.g. G.G. O'Collins, SJ, 'Spes Quaerens Intellectum', *Interpretation* 22 (1968), pp. 36-52 (38f.); C.E. Braaten, 'Toward a Theology of Hope', *Theology Today* 24 (1967–68), pp. 208-26; J. Macquarrie, 'Theologies of Hope: A Critical Examination', *Expository Times* 82 (1970–71), pp. 100-106 (104).
54 Cobb, 'What is the Future?', p. 3.
55 Zimmerli, 'Promise and Fulfilment', pp. 96f.
56 Moltmann, *Theology of Hope*, p. 104.
57 Meissner, 'Psychology of Hope', p. 120.
58 Zimmerli, 'Promise and Fulfilment', p. 95.
59 Moltmann, *Theology of Hope*, p. 104.
60 Moltmann, *Theology of Hope*, p. 105.
61 Moltmann, *Theology of Hope*, p. 105.
62 J.H. Kells, *Sophocles. Electra* (Cambridge: Cambridge University Press, 1973), p. 5.

To Chapter Eleven: Afterword

1 So John Barton, *Reading the Old Testament: Method in Biblical Study* (London: Darton, Longman & Todd, 1984) , pp. 136-37.
2 An unusual book in biblical studies, but one that was plainly inspired by this impulse in literature studies generally, was that of Edwin M. Good, *Irony in the Old Testament* (Philadelphia: Westminster, 1965; r.p. Bible and Literature Series, 3; Sheffield: Almond Press, 1981).
3 David M. Gunn, *The Story of King David: Genre and Interpretation* (Journal for the Study of the Old Testament Supplement Series, 6; Sheffield: JSOT Press, 1978); *The Fate of King Saul: An Interpretation of a Biblical Story* (Journal for the Study of the Old Testament Supplement Series, 14; Sheffield: JSOT Press, 1980).
4 See Brevard S. Childs, *Biblical Theology in Crisis* (Philadelphia: Westminster, 1970), and James Barr, 'Biblical Theology', in *Interpreter's Dictionary of the Bible. Supplementary Volume* (ed. K. Crim; Nashville: Abingdon, 1976), pp. 104-11.
5 I have outlined my thinking about postmodernism and the Hebrew Bible in my Presidential Address to the Society for Old Testament Study in 1996, 'The Pyramid and the Net: Old Testament Studies in a Postmodern Age'.
6 David J.A. Clines, *Interested Parties: The Ideology of Writers and Readers of the Hebrew Bible* (Journal for the Study of the Old Testament Supplement Series, 205; Gender, Culture, Theory, 1; Sheffield: Sheffield Academic Press, 1995), p. 190.
7 Phyllis Trible, 'Depatriarchalizing in Biblical Interpretation', *Journal of the American Academy of Religion* 41 (1973), pp. 30-48. See also John W. Miller, 'Depatriarchalizing God in Biblical Interpretation: A Critique',

Catholic Biblical Quarterly 48 (1986), pp. 609-16; and David J.A. Clines, 'What Does Eve Do to Help? and Other Irredeemably Androcentric Orientations in Genesis 1–3', in my *What Does Eve Do to Help? and Other Readerly Questions to the Old Testament* (Journal for the Study of the Old Testament Supplement Series, 94; Sheffield: JSOT Press, 1990), pp. 25-48.

8 I acknowledge here the influence of my colleague J. Cheryl Exum, not least in her *Fragmented Women: Feminist (Sub)versions of Biblical Narratives* (Journal for the Study of the Old Testament Supplement Series, 163; Sheffield: JSOT Press, 1993).

9 I have tried to sample the Hebrew Bible's views of masculinity in 'David the Man: The Construction of Masculinity in the Hebrew Bible', in *Interested Parties*, pp. 212-43, and in a forthcoming article, 'The Book of Psalms, Where Men Are Men: On the Gender of Hebrew Piety'.

10 My essays, 'The Ten Commandments, Reading from Left to Right' and 'Haggai's Temple, Constructed, Deconstructed and Reconstructed' (in *Interested Parties*, pp. 26-45 and 46-75 respectively) are examples of the political reading of texts I am speaking of here.

11 David J.A. Clines, *Job 1–20* (Word Biblical Commentary, 17; Waco, Texas: Word Books, 1990); vol. 2 is currently in preparation.

12 See especially my essay, 'Deconstructing the Book of Job', in *The Bible and Rhetoric: Studies in Biblical Persuasion and Credibility* (ed. Martin Warner; Warwick Studies in Philosophy and Literature; London: Routledge, 1990), pp. 65-80; and in *What Does Eve Do to Help? and Other Readerly Questions to the Old Testament*, pp. 106-23.

13 Clines, *Interested Parties*, pp. 18-19.

14 Clines, *Interested Parties*, p. 19.

15 See my essay, 'God in the Pentateuch: Reading against the Grain', in *Interested Parties*, pp. 187-211.

Bibliography

Albrektson, B. *History and the Gods: An Essay on the Idea of Historical Events as Divine Manifestations in the Ancient Near East and in Israel* (Lund: Gleerup, 1967).

Alonso Schökel, L. 'Hermeneutical Problems of a Literary Study of the Bible', *Congress Volume. Edinburgh 1974* (Supplements to Vetus Testamentum, 28; Leiden: E.J. Brill, 1975), pp. 1-15.

—*Narrative Structures in the Book of Judith* (The Center for Hermeneutical Studies in Hellenistic and Modern Culture. Protocol of the Eleventh Colloquy, ed. W. Wueller; Berkeley, CA, 1975).

Alter, R. 'A Literary Approach to the Bible', *Commentary* 60 (1975), pp. 70-77.

Anon. 'Editorial Responsibilities', *The Times Literary Supplement* (9 December, 1977), p. 1449.

Arend, W. *Die typischen Scenen bei Homer* (Berlin: Weidmann, 1933).

Barr, J. 'Biblical Theology', in *Interpreter's Dictionary of the Bible. Supplementary Volume* (ed. Keith Crim; Nashville: Abingdon, 1976), pp. 104-11.

—'Story and History in Biblical Theology', *Journal of Religion* 16 (1976), pp. 1-17.

Barthes, R. 'The Struggle with the Angel: Textual Analysis of Genesis 32:23-33', in R. Barthes *et al., Structural Analysis and Biblical Exegesis: Interpretational Essays* (Pittsburgh: Pickwick, 1974), pp. 21-33.

Barton, J. *Reading the Old Testament: Method in Biblical Study* (London: Darton, Longman & Todd, 1984).

Bassett, F.W. 'Noah's Nakedness and the Curse of Canaan', *Vetus Testamentum* 21 (1971), pp. 232-37.

Barnard, A.N. 'Was Noah a Righteous Man?', *Theology* 84 (1971), pp. 311-14.

Blenkinsopp, J. 'Theme and Motif in the Succession History (2 Sam xi 2ff) and the Yahwist Corpus', *Vetus Testamentum* 15 (1966), pp. 44-57.

—'The Structure of P', *Catholic Biblical Quarterly* 38 (1976), pp. 275-92.

—*et al., The Pentateuch* (Chicago; ACTA, 1971).

Bloch, E. *Das Prinzip Hoffnung* (Berlin: Aufbau-Verlag, 1954–59).

—*Man on His Own: Essays in the Philosophy of Religion* (New York: Herder & Herder, 1970).

Braaten, C.E. 'Toward a Theology of Hope', *Theology Today* 24 (1967–68), pp. 208-26.

Brueggemann, W. 'David and His Theologian', *Catholic Biblical Quarterly* 30 (1968), pp. 156-81.

—'The Kerygma of the "Priestly Writers"', *Zeitschrift für die alttestamentliche Wissenschaft* 84 (1972), pp. 397-414.

—*The Land: Place as Gift, Promise, and Challenge in Biblical Faith* (Philadelphia: Fortress Press, 1977).

Bibliography

Buber, M. *Moses: The Revelation and the Covenant* (Oxford: East and West Library, 1946).

Bultmann, R. '*Elpis, elpizo, ap-, proelpizo*', in *Theological Dictionary of the New Testament* (ed. G. Kittel and G. Friedrich; Grand Rapids: Eerdmans, 1964), II, pp. 517-35 (517-21).

Cassuto, U. *Commentary on Genesis* (Jerusalem; Magnes Press, 1961).

—'The Sequence and Arrangement of the Biblical Sections' [1947], in *Biblical and Oriental Studies* (Jerusalem: Magnes Press, 1973), I, pp. 1-6.

Childs, B.S. *Biblical Theology in Crisis* (Philadelphia: Westminster Press, 1970).

—*Exodus* (London: SCM Press, 1974).

—'The Exegetical Significance of Canon for the Study of the Old Testament', in *Congress Volume: Göttingen 1977* (ed. W. Zimmerli *et al.*; Supplements to Vetus Testamentum, 29; Leiden: E.J. Brill, 1978), pp. 66-80.

—'The Canonical Shape of the Prophetic Literature', *Interpretation* 32 (1978), pp. 46-55.

Clark, W.M. 'The Flood and the Structure of the Pre-patriarchal History', *Zeitschrift für die alttestamentliche Wissenschaft* 83 (1971), pp. 184-211.

Clements, R.E. *Abraham and David: Genesis XV and Its Meaning for Israelite Tradition* (Studies in Biblical Theology, II/5; London: SCM Press, 1967).

Clines, D.J.A. 'The Theology of the Flood Narrative', *Faith and Thought* 100 (1972–73), pp. 128-42.

—*I, He, We, and They: A Literary Approach to Isaiah 53* (Journal for the Study of the Old Testament Supplement Series, 1; Sheffield: JSOT Press, 1976).

—'What Does Eve Do to Help? and Other Irredeemably Androcentric Orientations in Genesis 1–3', in *What Does Eve Do to Help? and Other Readerly Questions to the Old Testament* (Journal for the Study of the Old Testament Supplement Series, 94; Sheffield: JSOT Press, 1990), pp. 25-48.

—'Deconstructing the Book of Job', in *The Bible and Rhetoric: Studies in Biblical Persuasion and Credibility* (ed. Martin Warner; Warwick Studies in Philosophy and Literature; London: Routledge, 1990), pp. 65-80; and in *What Does Eve Do to Help? and Other Readerly Questions to the Old Testament* (Journal for the Study of the Old Testament Supplement Series, 94; Sheffield: JSOT Press, 1990), pp. 106-23

—*Job 1–20* (Word Biblical Commentary, 17; Waco, Texas: Word Books, 1990).

—*Interested Parties: The Ideology of Writers and Readers of the Hebrew Bible* (Journal for the Study of the Old Testament Supplement Series, 205; Gender, Culture, Theory, 1; Sheffield: Sheffield Academic Press, 1995).

Coats, G.W. 'Conquest Traditions in the Wilderness Theme', *Journal of Biblical Literature* 95 (1976), pp. 177-90.

—*From Canaan to Egypt: Structural and Theological Context for the Joseph Story*

(Catholic Biblical Quarterly Monograph Series, 4; Washington, DC: Catholic Biblical Association of America, 1976).

Cobb, J.B., Jr. 'What is the Future? A Process Perspective', in *Hope and the Future of Man* (ed. Ewart H. Cousins; London: The Teilhard Centre for the Future of Man, 1972), pp. 1-14.

Cousins, E.H. (ed.). *Hope and the Future of Man* (London: The Teilhard Centre for the Future of Man, 1972).

Crossan, J.D. *The Dark Interval* (Niles, IL: Argus, 1975).

—(ed.), *Polyvalent Narration, Semeia* 9 (1977).

Dahlberg, B.T. 'On Recognizing the Unity of Genesis', *Theology Digest* 24 (1977), pp. 360-67.

de Pury, A. 'La Tour de Babel et la vocation d'Abraham: Notes exégétiques', *Etudes théologiques et religieuses* 53 (1978), pp. 80-97.

Davies, G.I. 'The Wilderness Itineraries: A Comparative Study', *Tyndale Bulletin* 25 (1974), pp. 46-81.

Dexinger, F. *Sturz der Gottersöhne oder Engel vor der Sintflut?* (Vienna: Herder, 1966).

Dorch, T.S. (ed. and trans.). *Classical Literary Criticism. Aristotle: On the Art of Poetry. Horace: On the Art of Poetry. Longinus: On the Sublime* (translated with an introduction by T.S. Dorch; Harmondsworth: Penguin, 1965).

Driver, S.R. *A Critical and Exegetical Commentary on Deuteronomy* (International Critical Commentary; Edinburgh: T. & T. Clark, 3rd edn, 1902).

de Vaulx, J. *Les Nombres* (Sources bibliques; Paris: Gabalda, 1972).

Eissfeldt, O. *The Old Testament: An Introduction* (trans. P.R. Ackroyd; Oxford: Blackwell, 1966).

Elliger, K. 'Sinn und Ursprung der priesterschriftlichen Geschichtserzählung', *Zeitschrift für Theologie und Kirche* 49 (1952), pp. 121-43.

Ellis, P.F. *The Yahwist: The Bible's First Theologian* (London: Chapman, 1969).

Exum, J.C. *Fragmented Women: Feminist (Sub)versions of Biblical Narratives* (Journal for the Study of the Old Testament Supplement Series, 163; Sheffield: JSOT Press, 1993).

Finkelstein, J.J. 'The Antediluvian Kings: A University of California Tablet', *Journal of Cuneiform Studies* 17 (1963), pp. 39-51

Fenik, B. *Typical Battle Scenes in the Iliad: Studies in the Narrative Techniques of Homeric Battle Description* (Wiesbaden: Steiner, 1968).

Fishbane, M.A. 'The Sacred Center: The Symbolic Structure of the Bible', in *Texts and Responses* (Festschrift Nahum N. Glatzer), ed. M.A. Fishbane and P.R. Flohr (Leiden: E.J. Brill, 1975), pp. 6-27.

Fohrer, G. *Introduction to the Old Testament* (trans. D. Green; London: SPCK, 1970).

Fretheim, T.E. *Creation, Fall and Flood: Studies in Genesis 1–11* (Minneapolis: Augsburg, 1969).

Forster, E.M. *Aspects of the Novel* (Harmondsworth: Penguin, 1962; originally published, 1927).

Gadamer, H.G. *Truth and Method* (New York: Seabury, 1975).
Gardner, H. *The Business of Criticism* (Oxford: Oxford University Press, 1959).
Goff, B.L. 'The Lost Yahwistic Account of the Conquest of Canaan', *Journal of Biblical Literature* 53 (1934), pp. 241-49.
Good, E.M. *Irony in the Old Testament* (Philadelphia: Westminster, 1965; r.p. Bible and Literature Series, 3; Sheffield: Almond Press, 1981).
Gray, G.B. *A Critical and Exegetical Commentary on Numbers* (International Critical Commentary; Edinburgh: T. & T. Clark, 1912).
Greimas, A.J. *Sémantique structurale: Recherche de méthode* (Paris: Larousse, 1966).
Gunkel, H. *Genesis* (Göttingen: Vandenhoeck & Ruprecht, 6th edn, 1964).
Gunn, D.M. 'Narrative Patterns and Oral Tradition in Judges and Samuel', *Vetus Testamentum* 24 (1974), pp. 286-317.
—'Traditional Composition in the "Succession Narrative"', *Vetus Testamentum* 26 (1976), pp. 214-29.
—*The Story of King David: Genre and Interpretation* (Journal for the Study of the Old Testament Supplement Series, 6; Sheffield: JSOT Press, 1978).
—*The Fate of King Saul: An Interpretation of a Biblical Story* (Journal for the Study of the Old Testament Supplement Series, 14; Sheffield: JSOT Press, 1980).
Gustafson, J.M. 'The Conditions of Hope: Reflections on Human Experience', *Continuum* 7 (1970), pp. 535-45.
Harrop, G.G. *Elijah Speaks Today: The Long Road into Naboth's Vineyard* (Nashville: Abingdon, 1975).
Hartman, T.C. 'Some Thoughts on the Sumerian King List and Genesis 5 and 11B', *Journal of Biblical Literature* 91 (1972), pp. 25-32.
Hauge, M.R. 'The Struggles of the Blessed in Estrangement', *Studia Theologica* 29 (1975), pp. 1-30, 113-46.
Hirsch, E.D. *Validity in Interpretation* (New Haven: Yale University Press, 1967).
Hoftijzer, J. *Die Verheissungen an die drei Erzväter* (Leiden: E.J. Brill, 1956).
Holzinger, H. *Genesis* (Kurzer Hand-Commentar zum Alten Testament; Freiburg: J.C.B. Mohr, 1898).
—*Numeri* (Kurzer Hand-Commentar zum Alten Testament: Tübingen: J.C.B. Mohr, 1903).
Humbert, P. 'Démesure et chute dans l'A.T.', in *maqqél shâqédh. La Branche d'amandier: Hommage à Wilhelm Vischer* (ed. S. Amsler *et al.*; Montpellier: Causse, Graille, Castelnau, 1960), pp. 63-82.
Jobling, D. *The Sense of Biblical Narrative: Three Structural Analyses in the Old Testament* (Journal for the Study of the Old Testament Supplement Series, 7; Sheffield: JSOT Press, 1978).
Johnson, M.D. *The Purpose of the Biblical Genealogies with Special Reference to the Setting of the Genealogies of Jesus* (Society for New Testament Studies Monograph Series, 8; Cambridge: Cambridge University Press, 1969).

Jones, H.O. 'The Concept of Story and Theological Discourse', *Scottish Journal of Theology* 29 (1976), pp. 415-33.

Kaiser, O. *Introduction to the Old Testament* (trans. J. Sturdy; Oxford: Blackwell, 1975).

Kells, J.H. *Sophocles. Electra* (Cambridge: Cambridge University Press, 1973).

Kennedy, A.R.S. *Leviticus and Numbers* (Century Bible; Edinburgh: T.C. & E.C. Jack, 1901).

Kidner, D. *Genesis* (Tyndale Old Testament Commentaries; London: Tyndale Press, 1967).

Kierkegaard, S. 'How to Derive True Benediction from Beholding Oneself in the Mirror of the Word', in *For Self-Examination. Proposed to this Age* (1851), in S. Kierkegaard, *For Self-Examination and Judge for Yourselves! and Three Discourses* (trans. W. Lowrie; London: Oxford University Press, 1946).

Kikawada, I.M. 'Two Notes on Eve', *Journal of Biblical Literature* 91 (1972), pp. 33-37.

Klaehn, T. *Die sprachliche Verwandschaft der Quelle K (2 Sam 9ff) der Samuelbücher mit J des Heptateuchs* (Borna-Leipzig: Noske, 1914).

Kline, M.G. 'Divine Kingship and Genesis 6:1-4', *Westminster Theological Journal* 24 (1962), pp. 187-204.

Koch, K. 'Ezra and the Origins of Judaism', *Journal of Semitic Studies* 19 (1974), pp. 173-97.

Korner, I.M. 'Hope as a Method of Coping', *Journal of Consultative and Clinical Psychology* 34 (1970), pp. 134-39.

Kuhn, T.S. *The Structure of Scientific Revolutions* (International Encyclopedia of Unified Sciences, vol. 2, no. 2; Chicago: Chicago University Press, 2nd edn, 1970).

Lakatos, I. and A. Musgrave (eds.). *Criticism and the Growth of Knowledge* (Proceedings of the International Colloquium in the Philosophy of Science, London, 1965, vol. 4; Cambridge: Cambridge University Press, 1970).

Levine, B.A. 'Numbers, Book of', in *Interpreter's Dictionary of the Bible. Supplementary Volume* (ed. K. Crim; Nashville: Abingdon, 1976), pp. 631-35.

Lord, A.B. 'Composition by Theme in Homer and Southslavic Epos', *Transactions of the American Philological Association* 82 (1951), pp. 71-80.

Louthan, S. 'The Practice of Hope', *Journal of Psychology and Theology* 2 (1974), pp. 276-83.

Macquarrie, J. 'Theologies of Hope: A Critical Examination', *Expository Times* 82 (1970–71), pp. 100-106.

Marcel, G. *Homo Viator: Introduction to a Metaphysic of Hope* (London: Gollancz, 1951).

McKenzie, J.L. 'Reflections on Wisdom', *Journal of Biblical Literature* 86 (1967), pp. 1-9.

Meissner, W.W., SJ. 'Notes on the Psychology of Hope', *Journal of Religion and Health* 12 (1973), pp. 7-29, 120-39.

Metz, J.B. 'Creative Hope', *Cross Currents* 17 (1967), pp. 171-79; reprinted in *New Theology* 5 (ed. M.E. Marty and D.G. Peerman; London: Macmillan, 1968), pp. 130-41.

—'The Future *Ex Memoria Passionis*', in *Hope and the Future of Man* (ed. Ewart H. Cousins; London: The Teilhard Centre for the Future of Man, 1972), pp. 116-31.

Miller, J.W. 'Depatriarchalizing God in Biblical Interpretation: A Critique', *Catholic Biblical Quarterly* 48 (1986), pp. 609-16.

Miller, P.D., Jr. *Genesis 1–11: Studies in Structure and Theme* (Journal for the Study of the Old Testament Supplement Series, 8; Sheffield: JSOT Press, 1978).

Miskotte, K.H. *When the Gods are Silent* (trans. John W. Doberstein; London: Collins, 1967).

Moltmann, J. 'Die Kategorie *Novum* in der christlichen Theologie', in *Ernst Bloch zu ehren* (ed. S. Unseld; Frankfurt: Suhrkamp, 1965), pp. 243-63.

—*Theology of Hope: On the Ground and Implications of a Christian Eschatology* (trans. James W. Leitch; London: SCM Press, 1967).

Navone, J. *Towards a Theology of Story* (Slough: St Paul Publications, 1977).

Noth, M. *A History of Pentateuchal Traditions* (trans. with an Introduction by Bernhard W. Anderson; Englewood Cliffs, NJ: Prentice–Hall, 1972).

O'Collins, G.G., SJ. 'Spes Quaerens Intellectum', *Interpretation* 22 (1968), pp. 36-52.

Palmer, R.E. *Hermeneutics: Interpretation Theory in Schleiermacher, Dilthey, Heidegger, and Gadamer* (Evanston: Northwestern University Press, 1969).

Pannenberg, W. 'The God of Hope', in *Basic Questions in Theology* (London: SCM Press, 1971), II, pp. 234-49 (ET of 'Der Gott der Hoffnung', in *Ernst Bloch zu ehren* [ed. S. Unseld; Frankfurt: Suhrkamp, 1965], pp. 209-25).

Pascal, B. *Pensées* (trans. J. Warrington; London: Dent, 1960).

Petersen, D.L. 'A Thrice-Told Tale: Genre, Theme, and Motif', *Biblical Research* 18 (1973), pp. 30-43.

—'The Yahwist on the Flood', *Vetus Testamentum* 26 (1976), pp. 438-46.

Polzin, R.M. *Biblical Structuralism: Method and Subjectivity in the Study of Ancient Texts* (Philadelphia: Fortress, and Missoula: Scholars Press, 1977).

Porter, J.R. *Leviticus* (Cambridge Bible Commentary; Cambridge: Cambridge University Press, 1976).

Pritchard, J.B. (ed.). *Ancient Near Eastern Texts Relating to the Old Testament* (Princeton: Princeton University Press, 2nd edn, 1955).

Rad, G. von. 'Ancient Word and Living Word: The Preaching of Deuteronomy and Our Preaching', *Interpretation* 15 (1961), pp. 3-13.

—*Theology of the Old Testament* (trans. D.M.G. Stalker; Edinburgh: Oliver &

Boyd, 1962, 1965).
—*The Problem of the Hexateuch and Other Essays* (trans. E. Trueman Dicken; Edinburgh: Oliver & Boyd, 1966).
—*Genesis: A Commentary* (trans. J.H. Marks; Philadelphia: Westminster, revised edn, 1972).
Reiner, E. 'The Etiological Myth of the Seven Sages', *Orientalia* 30 (1961), pp. 1-11.
Rendtorff, R. 'Genesis 8_{21} und die Urgeschichte des Jahwisten', *Kerygma und Dogma* 7 (1961), pp. 69-78.
—*Das überlieferungsgeschichtliche Problem des Pentateuchs* (Beihefte zur *Zeitschrift für die alttestamentliche Wissenschaft*, 147; Berlin: de Gruyter, 1977) (ET *The Problem of the Process of Transmission in the Pentateuch* [trans. J.J. Scullion; Journal for the Study of the Old Testament Supplement Series, 89; Sheffield: JSOT Press, 1990]).
Rice, G. 'The Curse that Never Was', *Journal of Religious Thought* 29 (1972), pp. 5-27.
Richter, W. 'Urgeschichte und Hoftheologie', *Biblische Zeitschrift* 10 (1966), pp. 96-105.
Ritschl, D. and H.O. Jones *'Story' als Rohmaterial der Theologie* (Theologische Existenz heute, 192; Munich: Chr. Kaiser, 1976).
Roth, R.P. *Story and Reality: An Essay on Truth* (Grand Rapids: Eerdmans, 1973).
Sawyer, J.F.A. *From Moses to Patmos: New Perspectives in Old Testament Study* (London: SPCK, 1977).
Scholes, R. and R. Kellogg. *The Nature of Narrative* (New York: Oxford University Press, 1966).
Schmid, H.H. *Der sogennante Jahwist* (Zurich: Theologischer Verlag, 1976).
Seale, M.S. 'Numbers xiii.32', *Expository Times* 68 (1956–57), p. 28.
Shipley, J.T. (ed.). *Dictionary of World Literature* (Totowa, NJ: Littlefield, Adams & Co., 1968).
Skinner, J. *A Critical and Exegetical Commentary on Genesis* (International Critical Commentary; Edinburgh: T. & T. Clark, 2nd edn, 1930).
Snaith, N.H. *Leviticus. Numbers* (New Century Bible; London: Nelson, 1967).
Soisalon-Soininen, I. 'Die Urgeschichte im Geschichtswerk des Jahwisten', *Temenos* 6 (1970), pp. 130-41.
Speiser, E.A. *Genesis* (Anchor Bible; New York: Doubleday, 1964).
Steck, O.H. 'Genesis 12:1-3 und die Urgeschichte des Jahwisten', in *Probleme biblischer Theologie. Gerhard von Rad zum 70. Geburtstag* (ed. H.W. Wolff; Munich: Chr. Kaiser, 1971), pp. 525-54.
Storm, H. *Seven Arrows* (New York: Ballantine, 1973).
Stotland, E. *The Psychology of Hope* (San Francisco: Jossey–Bass, 1969).
Sturdy, J. *Numbers* (Cambridge Bible Commentary; Cambridge: Cambridge University Press, 1976).

Thompson, M. and R. *Critical Reading and Writing* (New York: Random House, 1969).
Thrall, W.F. and A. Hibberd. *A Handbook to Literature* (New York: Odyssey, 1960).
Towers, B. *Teilhard de Chardin* (London: Lutterworth, 1966)
Trible, P. 'Depatriarchalizing in Biblical Interpretation', *Journal of the American Academy of Religion* 41 (1973), pp. 30-48.
Van Seters, J. *Abraham in History and Tradition* (New Haven: Yale University Press, 1975).
Weiser, A. *Introduction to the Old Testament* (trans. D.M. Barton; London: Darton, Longman & Todd, 1961).
Wellhausen, J. *Die Composition des Hexateuchs* (Berlin: Reimer, 1899).
—*Prolegomena to the History of Ancient Israel* (New York: Meridian, r.p. 1957).
Westermann, C. 'Arten der Erzählung in der Genesis', in his *Forschung am Alten Testament* (Munich: Chr. Kaiser, 1964), pp. 9-91.
—*Genesis* (Biblischer Kommentar: Altes Testament, 1/1; Neukirchen: Neukirchener Verlag, 1966).
—'Promises to the Patriarchs', in *Interpreter's Dictionary of the Bible. Supplementary Volume* (ed. K. Crim; Nashville: Abingdon, 1976), pp. 690-93.
—*Die Verheissungen an die Väter: Studien zur Vätergeschichte* (Forschungen zur Religion und Literatur des Alten und Neuen Testaments, 116; Göttingen: Vandenhoeck & Ruprecht, 1976).
Wharton, J.A. 'The Occasion of the Word of God: An Unguarded Essay on the Character of the Old Testament as the Memory of God's Story with Israel', *Austin Seminary Bulletin: Faculty Edition* 84 (Sept. 1968), pp. 3-54.
Wilson, R.R. *Genealogy and History in the Biblical World* (New Haven: Yale University Press, 1977).
Wink, W. *The Bible in Human Transformation: Toward a New Paradigm for Biblical Study* (Philadelphia: Fortress, 1973).
—'On Wrestling with God: Using Psychological Insights in Biblical Study', *Religion in Life* 47 (1978), pp. 136-47.
Wolff, H.W. 'The Kerygma of the Yahwist', *Interpretation* 20 (1966) pp. 131-58, originally published in *Evangelische Theologie* 24 (1964), pp. 73-97.
—'The Elohistic Fragments in the Pentateuch', *Interpretation* 26 (1972), pp. 158-73, originally published in *Evangelische Theologie* 27 (1969), pp. 59-72.
Zimmerli, W. 'Promise and Fulfilment', in *Essays on Old Testament Interpretation* (ed. C. Westermann; London: SCM Press, 1963), pp. 89-122.
—*Man and His Hope in the Old Testament* (Studies in Biblical Theology, II/20; London: SCM Press, 1971: originally published 1968).
Zweig, P. *The Adventurer* (London: Dent, 1974).

Index of Biblical References

Index of Biblical References

Index of Subjects